MW00978973

HISTORIC
GUYSBOROUGH
A PORTRAIT OF HOME

*To Rick with fond memories
and hope for the future.*
John

JOHN N. GRANT

John N. Grant

Nimbus Publishing Limited
PO Box 9166
Halifax, NS B3K 5M8
(902) 455-4286

Printed and bound in Canada

Design: Terri Strickland

Front cover: The British House, on Main Street, c.1900, see page 67.
Title page: Three people viewing barquentine anchored in Guysborough Harbour, NSARM

Library and Archives Canada Cataloguing in Publication

    Grant, John N.
    Historic Guysborough / John N. Grant.
    Includes bibliographical references.
    ISBN 1-55109-481-9

1. Guysborough (N.S.)—History—Pictorial works. I. Title.

FC2349.G89G73 2004   971.6'21   C2004-903611-4

We acknowledge the financial support of the Government of Canada through the Book Publishing Industry Development Program (BPIDP) and the Canada Council for our publishing activities.

⊱ *Dedication* ⊰

This work is dedicated to the memory of my parents, C. Wilkie Grant (1912–1991)
from Beaver Mountain, Antigonish County, and Jean A. (Gardner) Grant (1911–2000)
of Halifax.

My father came to Guysborough as a young lawyer to establish an independent practice
and my mother joined him. Both became deeply involved with the church, the school,
and the community, making Guysborough home for themselves and their four children.

This work is further dedicated to my aunts: Jean (Grant) Finlayson, Dorothy (Gardner)
Jones (1916–1998), and Marion Gardner.

Acknowledgements

The greatest fear in acknowledging the assistance received in the preparation of any such work is that someone might be omitted. If I have made this error, I beg your indulgence and hope that you accept my appreciation in another form.

I have first to thank my brother and consultant, Jamie, for his great interest in and knowledge of the history of Guysborough. He remained constantly and consistently helpful through numerous telephone calls and visits and offered his personal store of knowledge including some great stories—which in many cases, unfortunately, could not be included here. Nonetheless, his influence on this work is reflected on every page.

Thanks also to my sister Margaret, who helped to push the project forward by her interest, support, and photography.

Special thanks to Debbie MacIssac and Debbie Burns who typed the manuscript and brought it to a presentable form.

I relied upon two institutions especially: the Nova Scotia Archives and Record Management and the Old Court House Museum (Guysborough). Archivists Garry Shutlak and Virginia Clark and curator Kim Avery looked after me very kindly. Other institutions to which I owe appreciation include the Anglican Diocesan Archives, the Acadia University Archives, the Dalhousie University Library and Archives, the St. Francis Xavier University Archives, the Maritime Museum of the Atlantic, the Art Gallery of Nova Scotia, the Cambridge Military Library, and the Black Cultural Centre.

Many individuals have also responded to my pleas for assistance, including Dr. Alan Marble, Betty MacIntosh, Eldon Halloran, Peter Jackson, Paul Long, Ainley Clyke, Leland Williams, Victor and Florence Shea, Margaret George, Dianne Tulk, Mark Haynes, Don Armstrong, Marie MacMaster, Jim Drysdale, Charles MacKeen, Harold Grant, Jeanne Howell, Rob MacIlreith, the Francheville family, Henry Bishop, John Sullivan, John Hall, Lynn-Marie Richard, and Christopher Cook.

Thanks to Nimbus Publishing for the opportunity to tell this story and to Dorothy Blythe, managing editor Sandra McIntyre, freelance copy editor Christine Lovelace, and Penelope Jackson, for their marked contribution to Historic Guysborough.

While I willingly share any positive comments this work may receive with all the above, I must accept the responsibility for any errors or deficiencies. It has been a pleasure to make this contribution to telling the story of home.

Contents

Introduction

Although Guysborough's first encounters with humankind are lost in the mists of time, it is known that the area became a minor crossroad in the history of the North Atlantic world. The ancient peoples of the East Coast hunted this land, lived in the shelter of its shores, and travelled the length of Chedabucto, the Mi'kmaw name for the bay into which Guysborough Harbour empties. Europeans also came early to these shores.

While contesting authorities still seek physical evidence and argue their claims, many believe that Prince Henry Sinclair, Earl of the Orkneys, landed close to Guysborough Harbour in 1398 and explored the area. Some say Sinclair was a latecomer, crediting the tales of St. Brendan and the Irish Monks, who supposedly braved the Western Ocean to escape the ravages of the Northmen.

The Vikings are also connected with the Guysborough area. The discovery of a Norse axe nearby in 1880 might suggest that visitors from L'Anse aux Meadows explored the area around the year 1000. It is certain, however, that European fishermen knew Guysborough Harbour long before 1600, and likely found refuge there. Jean Denys of Honfleur published a chart of his explorations of the region in 1506, and 101 years later French explorers Samuel de Champlain and Marc Lescarbot visited a Basque fishing station in "Tor Bay," about twenty kilometres from Guysborough. Its proprietor, Captain Savalet, informed Champlain that he had been using the site for forty-two years. Savalet was probably not the only European fisherman taking advantage of the richness of the local fishery.

Guysborough Harbour proved to be too attractive to be used simply as an occasional refuge or a base for the summer fishery. The snug, safe harbour, its attendant river, and its proximity to the more extensive Salmon River system, combined with a convenient bluff guarding access to its narrow entrance, made it an ideal location for trade.

Sir William Alexander was granted land in 1621 by King James to fulfill his dream of a "New Scotland." In 1629, following his capture of Sir William Alexander's colony in Cape Breton, Captain Charles Daniel built his trading post and shore base at Chedabucto (Guysborough), which he later relinquished to Isaac de Razilly; at de Razilly's death it passed to Nicholas Denys. Denys was a French fur trader, merchant, and settler who constructed a stockade, armed and manned it, and undertook to hold it against his enemies (both French and English), using it as one of the centres of his mercantile empire. He exported the first sawed lumber from Canada, traded with the Mi'kmaq for furs, fished, rendered oil from sea mammals, and encouraged the growing of crops. The height of his development in Chedabucto was marked by the employment of about 120 men and the clearing of twenty acres of land for crops outside his armed stockade.

After 1682, however, a new regime was in charge of Chedabucto, and Sieur Bergier, a Huguenot merchant from La Rochelle, further developed the site under the authority of the Trading Company of Acadia. Sieur Bergier replaced the stockade, built a chapel in honour of St. Louis, patron saint of Chedabucto, and increased the agricultural development of the cleared lands. In addition, a wind-powered sawmill was constructed, and a cluster of houses was built along the harbour edge toward the present site of Guysborough.

Chedabucto proved to be an attractive prize and in 1688 it was captured and looted by English pirates operating out of Boston, but the little centre was soon rebuilt, and for some time it represented the apex of the authority of France on the mainland of Nova Scotia.

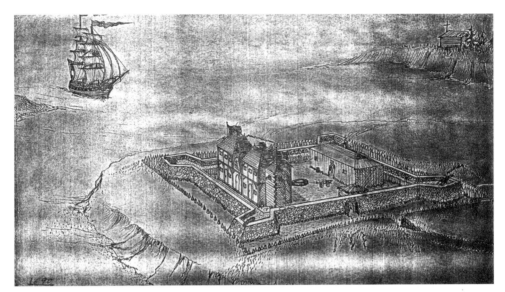

"FORT ST. LOUIS À CHEDABUCTOU, 1690," AS DRAWN BY ARCHITECT AND HISTORIAN MARK HAYNES.

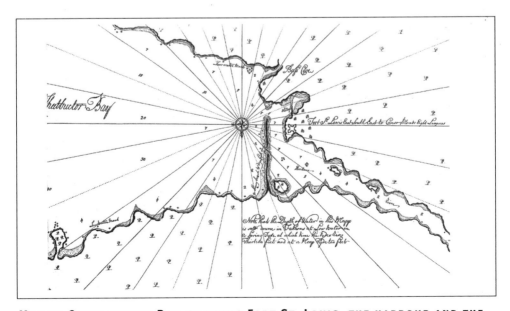

MAP OF CHEDABUCTOU BAY, SHOWING FORT ST. LOUIS, THE HARBOUR AND THE RIVER AT WHAT IS NOW GUYSBOROUGH, C.1690.

Harriet Cunningham Hart's prize-winning essay, "History of the County of Guysborough" (1877), supplies a description of the fortification built by Bergier: "In 1685 his establishment consisted of two buildings, 60 feet front by 20 in depth. There were 33 persons residing there, having provisions for a year. They had four cannon besides guns, pistols and halberds, 240 bushels of salt, a bark of thirty tons, fifteen shallops, and everything requisite for the fishery."

Saint-Vallier expressed optimism for the future of the community of "50 Frenchmen" and advocated "a company of soldiers," especially if some were fishermen, labourers, and craftsmen, to be stationed there. His views must have been supported by Jacques De Meulles, the Intendant of New France who also visited the community in 1686, for in 1687 a small number of additional troops were added to the defence of the nascent settlement. Meanwhile, the power of France was under attack throughout North America, and not even Count Frontenac—"the Father of New France" and its only governor to visit Guysborough, or indeed Acadia (French Nova Scotia)—could adequately prepare the station for protracted warfare. In 1690, troops acting under the authority of Sir William Phips of Massachusetts attacked Acadia and captured Port-Royal.

Phips then ordered two of his captains to attack the remaining French settlements in Nova Scotia. Captain John Alden was to concentrate his efforts within the Bay of Fundy. Captain Cyprian Southack, on the other hand, was to sail to Chedabucto in an expedition designed to drive the French competitors of the Massachusetts fishermen from Nova Scotia waters, and in June 1690, Fort St. Louis à Chedabuctou fell. Southack left a fascinating account of his attack on the little community in a letter to his father:

We sallied up at the Fort at Once and they killed me three men, and wounded me six, so we fought them Six houres, and they beat us off from the Fort, and about pistol shot from the Fort, we gott into a Great house, where I found 4 barrells of Gun Powder, and I made fire balls and Arrows, and we sallied up againe to the Trenches, and there got in my self with 4 men more, so that their Great Guns could not hurt us, and we threw severall balls into the Fort, at last it got into the House of Guard and set Fire, and in One houres time the Fort was all on Fire. And then the Govr struck the Flag, and he with his Souldiers and the Priests came out, and then the fort in One half houres time blew up with the Powder that was in it…so I was 5 days demolishing of it which the Governor now informs me stood the French King 3000 sterling within these two years which was built of stone and plaster of Paris and trenched around.

PIERRE-ESPRIT RADISSON

Pierre-Esprit Radisson, the French Canadian trader who would become responsible in part for the creation of the British Hudson Bay Company, visited the establishment at Chedabucto in 1662.

The Phips expedition has been described as an affair of "pure pillage"; certainly the uncontrolled plundering by Phips' Massachusetts troops after the capitulation of Port Royal, and later Chedabucto, supports this description.

Thanks to Count Frontenac, who would not surrender Quebec to the British, Nova Scotia remained a French possession despite the English victories. Spanning over one hundred years of conflict for empire in the Americas, the British captured Acadia in 1613, 1629, 1654, 1690 and 1710. Following the first four conflicts, France regained with diplomacy what they had lost in war. However, by the Treaty of Utrecht in 1713, Acadia, within its "ancient limits," became a British possession. Cape Breton Island (Isle Royale) remained part of the French Empire and soon bristled with the firepower of the Fortress of Louisbourg.

The years between the 1690s and the 1780s used to be viewed as blank pages in the history of Guysborough. However, the recent work of historian Mark Haynes has shed light on this murky period, revealing that there was much more activity than previously believed. While the Massachusetts expedition carried out its mission of destruction and plunder, there is nothing to suggest that the settlers outside of the fort were removed or deprived of their lands. However, despite the apparent reconstruction of the fort, it is very likely that the importance of Chedabucto declined. The name itself disappears from the census records of the early eighteenth century, but it is likely that French settlers remained, and both English and French fishermen again made use of the harbour. In 1720, Governor Richard Phillips stationed three companies of his troops in Canso, and constructed a fort there. W. S. MacNutt asserts that by this time, Canso had become "by far the most important commercial centre in Nova Scotia." The waters of Chedabucto Bay continued to be visited by some of the "ninety six sail of English and 200 French" that Captain Benjamin Young of His Majesty's ship Rose reported in his 1720 visit to Canso. Without doubt, at least some of these ships and men visited Chedabucto as well.

Haynes contends that the deportation of the Acadians from Nova Scotia in the years between 1755 and 1763 did not involve Guysborough because the Acadians there had already sworn an oath of loyalty to the crown. In 1764, there were only fourteen Acadian families at Chedabucto. It is not known if they were residents or refugees, or if they were alone, or joined others already there. We are told that they had cleared land, engaged in the summer fishery, and built and sold fishing boats to their compatriots on Cape Breton Island. The English-speaking settlers who arrived in force in the 1780s made reference to an old French cross marking an Acadian cemetery, to the ruins of French cellars, and to the remnants of forges where iron had been worked by the Acadian blacksmiths. These few remains marked the end of the French occupancy of Guysborough.

English settlers at Chedabucto either came hard on the heels of the departing French or, more likely, overlapped with them. Certainly by 1780 there was the small English settlement of Milford in the area, and at least one English settler lived on the shores of Guysborough Harbour itself. Tradition maintains that at least some of the New England Planters who made up the "old families" had been introduced to the area as a result of the 1745 capture of the mighty French Fortress of Louisbourg. The fortification was a threat to the New England fishery and an impediment to trade between British America and the motherland. Consequently, by 1744 relations between Great Britain and France had again deteriorated into war, and New England seized their opportunity to eliminate the threat. Proposed by William Shirley, Governor of Massachusetts, and led by William Pepperell, an army of citizen soldiers was raised in New England to attack Louisbourg with economic cause, military zeal, and religious fervour. Canso was the rendezvous point, where the new army was drilled in preparation for the attack on the walls of Louisbourg. It was then that a member of the Hadley family who was a captain of one of the transport ships that carried the troops to Canso and then to Louisbourg became familiar with the prospects in the Chedabucto Bay area. The date of his move to Milford Haven is unclear, but a daughter of the extended family appears to have been born there as early as 1768. By 1781, Joseph

Hadley and his family were living there year round on lands reserved to him in 1764 and confirmed by grant on October 1, 1784. The lands of the other pre-Loyalist families who lived outside the limits of Guysborough Harbour were likewise protected.

After some years of a precarious and cautious existence, in a time when every unknown ship might carry enemies and any unwary move might mean death, the lives of the Cooks, Hortons, Ingersalls, Pearts, Callahans, Godfreys, Tobys, Hadleys, and others were changed forever by the arrival of the Kings Transports in 1784. They were well aware of, and affected by, the war raging in the colonies between those loyal to King George III and those who wished to separate from the British Empire. The war had been brought to their doorstep when Canso was destroyed by John Paul Jones, operating under the authority of George Washington and the Continental Congress. They were no doubt also aware of the decisive October 1781 Battle of Yorktown and of the 1783 Treaty of Versailles, which brought an end to the hostilities.

The end of the hostilities, however, was not the beginning of peace for the thousands of persons who became the political refugees of the American Revolution. While the majority of Loyalists stayed in the new United States, many found it safer to leave. Loyalists' homes were attacked, their jobs lost, and their access to legal protection denied. After 1777 the United States banished prominent Loyalists, and everywhere Loyalists ran the risk of violence. For many—despite the challenges of pioneer settlement—the choice was not whether but where to go, and the Loyalists expected compensation for their losses in the cause of loyalty. The Loyalists came from every level of colonial life. The majority were farmers, but a sizeable minority were office holders, businessmen, and professionals. Artisans, merchants, servants, shopkeepers, innkeepers, labourers, sailors, lawyers, teachers, doctors, and clergymen were also represented in the Loyalist ranks. There were more poor than rich, and many different kinds of minorities were represented. Their ranks were swelled by British troops (both English and German speaking). Approximately thirty-five thousand of them, including some thirty-five hundred free African Americans, came to Nova Scotia, and it was they who created modern Guysborough.

On May 16, 1784, the transport Content arrived at Chedabucto from Halifax. It carried one hundred and forty-nine officers and men (but very few women and children) of the Duke of Cumberland's regiment. The ship moved through the narrow entrance where, other than the home of Captain Joseph Hadley and the fields of the old French settlement, there was no sign of human presence amid the uninterrupted forest, from skyline to water line; the prospect of hard labour loomed before them. Others soon joined them. By mid-June, the Associated Departments of the Army and Navy, the 60th Regiment, and the Augustine Loyalists had all made their way to the new settlement. Surveyors and their assistants were busy with chain and rod, marking out land lots to accommodate the new settlers. Little Island became a depot for supplies maintained by Colonel Molleson and the remnant of the 71st Regiment.

A neat town was laid out, streets were created and land cleared. Construction kept everyone busy, as homes had to be finished before the onset of winter. Wharves and piers were built for the fishery and for trade. The shire town was first referred to as New Manchester, but those who wished to honour Sir Guy Carleton, their former military leader and later Commander-in-Chief of His Majesty's forces in North America, outnumbered those who wished to recall the patronage of Lord Manchester, and the town's name became Guysborough.

By then the ethnic character of Guysborough was essentially in place. The majority of the inhabitants were English-speaking Christians from the British Isles, representing the Anglican, Baptist, Methodist, Presbyterian, and Roman Catholic denominations. German-

SIR WILLIAM CAMPBELL, GUYSBOROUGH LOYALIST AND UPPER CANADIAN SUPREME COURT JUDGE, C.1820S

William Campbell (1758–1834) was one of the settlers who came to Guysborough with the Loyalists. Born in Caithness, Scotland, Campbell joined the British military and served in North America during the American Revolutionary War. Following the war, he worked as a quartermaster with the Associated Departments of the Army and Navy, and he was with them when they re-established themselves at Guysborough on Chedabucto Bay in 1784. Campbell had talent and ambition, and played a prominent role in the life of the new township. He studied law with Thomas Cutler, a Yale graduate and Loyalist immigrant, and held various local offices. He represented his district as MLA and in turn became attorney general, councillor, and coal contractor of Cape Breton Island during its years as a separate colony. He was later appointed a judge in the colony of Upper Canada (Ontario) and eventually became its chief justice. Upon retirement he received his highest honour: he was knighted.

There is a romantic touch to Campbell's story as well. Upon the 1784 arrival of his transport ship off Guysborough Harbour, he prepared to go ashore in a small boat to engage a pilot. As he readied to go over the side, he spied a girl working among the fish flakes on the beach. Responding to the cautionary teasing of his fellow travellers, he playfully replied that he was going to meet his future wife. His prophecy was fulfilled, as the Township Book recorded that "William Campbell married to Hannah Hadley 1 June 1785." Hannah Hadley was the daughter of one of the original settlers. Their story is preserved by Campbell House Museum in Toronto, Ontario.

---

speaking settlers were soon joined by Irish Newfoundlanders, who settled along the coast with some of the returned Acadians. There were also settlers of African descent, some of whom came to Guysborough as Loyalists, and some as slaves.

The military groups that settled in the area contained many officers, a situation that boded well for Guysborough. They provided leadership to the community and insisted that their children have the advantages of their class; as a result, schools were deemed a necessary part of the village. The civilian Loyalists included individuals of all levels in society and contributed to the fortunes of the community, which in 1788 boasted two hundred and twenty-five families. Some families and individuals left to seek their fortunes elsewhere, while others arrived for the same purpose. The community gradually developed cohesion through intermarriage between military and civilians, between Loyalists and the original settlers.

Although the end of the American Revolution had forced the emigrants into what some called Nova Scarcity, it provided them with the opportunity for economic growth. For some years the Americans were excluded from the local fishery and not allowed to trade with the important markets of the British West Indies. The authorities hoped that this trade would become the basis for Maritime prosperity. The single crop economies of these islands needed timber, fish and a myriad of other items. While their need proved to be greater than the maritime pioneer economies could supply, they provided a ready market for the aspirations of many a Nova Scotian entrepreneur, including those in Guysborough.

The years around the turn of the eighteenth century were dominated by the search for economic stability that emerged from a renewal of war. The demand of the mother country for colonial goods of every kind, including fish and timber, provided a welcome market for the lumbermen, fishermen, and ship builders of Guysborough. Likewise, as Britain and the United States moved closer to the War of 1812, British colonial trade became even more important as suppliers in the United States were cut off.

When President James Madison of the United States declared war on Great Britain, the effect was felt in Guysborough. The militia was reorganized throughout the province, and Guysborough's defences were not excluded. The site of the old French fort was rearmed with British cannons sent from Halifax, and a sergeant of the British Army arrived to reorganize the defences. H. C. Hart writes that "some wooden buildings were erected on the Point, and an embankment of earth thrown up around the top of the bluff, with embrasures for the cannon."

Local government was established by 1785, and a courthouse, jail, and other public buildings constructed. Because the sea was always perilous, provision was made for the construction of roads. In 1787, the local government decreed "that the beaches or shores of Milford Haven River, from its eastern entrance to the head of the tide, shall be considered a public road, and all trees and bushes there shall be considered a nuisance on said highway." The following year it was ordered that a road be created from Chedabucto to Dorchester (Guysborough to Antigonish). Within a few years, roads to the "settlements at the Strait of Canso" and to Musquodoboit, which connected to Halifax, were also started. However, the gale of 1811 left these rough trails blocked by fallen trees. Roads were established because of the dangers and challenges of travel by water, but the difficulty of travel by land often left the sea as the only option. Consequently, there was interest and support for the establishment of regular packet boats between Guysborough and Arichat (later Guysborough and Mulgrave), and between Guysborough and Halifax, to maintain contact with the outside world.

By the early 1830s, Guysborough was taking on the form that we recognize today. In 1831, a young Joseph Howe travelled the province to sell subscriptions to his newspaper and collect money owed to him. He visited Guysborough and published accounts of his expedition in a series of articles he called "Eastern Rambles." After expressing his disappointment with both Sherbrooke and Antigonish, he described his entry to Guysborough as "shrouded in mist and smothered in showers" and found lodging at the inn of Christian Miller (or Müller). Despite the rain, Howe expressed his delight with the natural setting of the village and wrote:

> Indeed every step you take—every turn of the eye—furnishes some new combination of land and water, some scenic grace that was not at first observed; and the result of the whole survey satisfies the Traveler that there are few places in the Province whose natural beauties and great commercial advantages are more agreeably blended.

Howe described the community as consisting of "an Episcopal Church, a Roman Catholic Chapel, a Methodist Meeting [House], a Court House, and some schools." There were also thirty to forty residences, and a great many stores, barns, and outhouses. Howe described a few of the stores as "roomy and extensive," and pointed to several good wharves "at which vessels of heavy tonnage may be accommodated." Howe also praised the villagers for the "tasty arrangement" of their gardens and complimented them on both the vegetables and the flowers they produced. Howe further complimented the women of Guysborough on the quality of the "delicious currant wine" they brewed, and praised the community for "being frank, intelligent, and hospitable." There can be little doubt that this combination of wine and good conversation was dear to Howe's heart.

Just two years earlier, Thomas Chandler Haliburton commented on the economic prospects of the community in his History of Nova Scotia (which Howe published in 1829). He noted that the fisheries of Chedabucto Bay were among the most productive in the world, and that "cod fish, pollock, herring, and mackerel" were taken in great number and sometimes entered Guysborough Harbour in such quantities that several thousand barrels could be caught in one day. As much as Haliburton praised the fishery, he lamented that it had caused agriculture to be ignored. Nonetheless, he commented on the "spontaneous fertility of the soil" which allowed the inhabitants to raise considerable numbers of black cattle, horses, and sheep, as well as producing great quantities of butter. Though fish and fish oil were the community's major exports, they were supplemented by others: several cargoes of livestock were exported to Newfoundland each year, and butter and some surplus of potatoes and oats also made it to other markets. By the third decade of the 1800s, the earlier trade in hewn and sawn lumber was in decline, as the easily accessible woodland had been harvested, and the British government gradually reduced their subsidy of colonial timber.

While historians and newspapermen wrote about Guysborough, life went on much as usual in the village during the 1830s. Children went to school and Sunday school, they worked and played and joined the youth divisions of organizations like the Guysborough and Manchester Total Abstinence Society (1830). Their parents worked, commented on the relocation of the post office (1832), noted Joseph Howe's libel trial (1835) and the formation of the County of Guysborough (1836), read about the Battle of the Alamo (1836) in their newspaper, tut-tutted the rebellions of 1837–1838 in Upper and Lower Canada, and celebrated the coronation of Queen Victoria with, H. C. Hart reports, a "general illumination" and "numerous appropriate mottoes and devices" on the night of June 28, 1838.

Perhaps the most scandalous and newsworthy local event occurred in 1833 when riots occurred in Canso and Fox Island. The hair was cut off the mane and tail of a visiting priest's horse; some saw this as a deliberate insult to Roman Catholics, and hot tempers led to civil disturbance. The residents of the shire town were no doubt alarmed at the events, consternated by the apparent role of Father James Grant, a Guysborough-based parish priest, and concerned about their personal safety. Relief likely greeted the capture of the ringleaders, their subsequent trial, and especially the removal of most of them to a Halifax prison from the Guysborough jail.

The 1840s and 1850s were generally prosperous years for Nova Scotia. The post-war slump following the end of the Napoleonic and American wars had been endured, and the economic panic that had accompanied the British decision to embrace free trade had been weathered. In 1854, the province became part of a British North American reciprocal trade agreement with the United States that allowed free trade in natural products. The eager markets of the growing industrial centres of New England provided opportunities for Nova Scotia businessmen who rushed to fill the American shopping basket. The export of products, however, was also accompanied by an export of Nova Scotians, as first a trickle and then a flood of young people sought the economic attractions of the "Boston States."

Meanwhile, other changes and challenges were occurring. When the Civil War (1861–1865) between the North and South broke out in the United States, trade flourished. The competition for the fisheries between the white sails of the American fishermen and the tanned sails of the Nova Scotians declined, and control fell by default to the locals, as the American war effort consumed manpower and ships alike. The American government, however, in an effort to divert attention from their internal problems, announced that they were going to cancel the trade agreement, prompting some Americans to look northward once again with thoughts of expanding the United States. This potential military threat, made real by the Fenian raids into British North America a few short years later, caused the reorganization of the Nova Scotia Militia, as it seemed young men might once again be called upon to defend their province. In Guysborough, the volunteer company, the Chedabucto Greys, was organized in the winter of 1860. The sixty officers and men of this unit purchased the old Town Hall for use as a drill room and, as H. C. Hart explains, used a smaller room for an armoury where "the well-kept Enfield rifles presented a very warlike appearance." Drilled and practised in target shooting, the Greys became a central point of local society. Entertainment was conducted for their support, dinners were held, mock battles undertaken, and promotions were sought and broadcast. Fortunately, hostilities with the United States were averted and the militia companies were disbanded until the next beating of the imperial drums of war.

By this time Guysborough likely closely resembled the model Douglas Francis used in Origins to describe the region. He wrote:

> By the mid-nineteenth century the three maritime colonies had come of age economically and politically. Eight out of every nine people in the region had been born there. But the inhabitants were far from homogeneous. Religious, ethnic, and provincial divisions remained, particularly among the groups pushed to the margins of Maritime Society, like the Micmacs [sic] and Blacks, and to a lesser extent the Acadians. Regional loyalties also were strong. Many Maritimers were skeptical of the possibilities of Maritime union when politicians first seriously discussed the idea in the early 1860s. The idea of Union with the Canadas seemed even more remote.

Political change, however, was underway. The Province of Canada (1841–1867)—today's Ontario and Quebec—was experiencing internal political problems and saw a wider union as a solution. In 1864, the Canadian guests at the Charlottetown Conference seized the initiative and convinced many of the Maritimers there to support a union of British North America instead. Premier Charles Tupper, later Sir Charles Tupper, was among those convinced, and he worked to make Nova Scotia part of the new union. Tupper carefully avoided defeat by not allowing the voters to express their opinion by way of the ballot box. In 1867, however, Nova Scotians expressed their disapproval by soundly defeating most of the supporters of Confederation in both the provincial and federal elections held simultaneously that year. In Guysborough, anti-confederation petitions were signed and sent to Halifax, and anti-confederates were elected to the provincial Legislative Assembly and to the federal House of Commons. There was some satisfaction in using the polls to express their displeasure over what was considered by many to be an illegal change in the province's constitution.

In 1871, some Guysboroughians, either latently or blatantly anti-confederate, seized an opportunity to strike back at the Canadians. Many a Guysborough area boy was employed on American-owned fishing vessels, and many a local merchant had his income supplemented by the American trade. While in the normal course of events locals were very protective of their fishing grounds, the story of the *E.A. Horton* was widely appreciated. The Gloucester, Massachusetts, based Horton loaded with mackerel, apparently caught legally, was lying just off-shore while its captain was ashore. Meanwhile, the ship's cook was hand-lining for cod for dinner when the Canadian fishery patrol frigate Sweepstakes, under the command of Captain James Torrey of Guysborough, sailed by. Caught fishing in Canadian waters, the crew was arrested and the *Horton* taken into Guysborough Harbour. Its sails and running gear were stripped and locked away, and it was tied up at a local wharf under guard. The *Horton's* captain was, however, not easily discouraged and vowed he would recapture his vessel. With the help of some locals, he reassembled his crew in a nearby warehouse, smuggled them aboard, obtained the rigging, and fled the harbour on a stormy Sunday night in October. Pursued by fishery patrol boats, the *Horton* nonetheless made it safely back to its homeport and a hero's welcome. American newspapers soon arrived in Guysborough with headlines celebrating the escape of the *Horton*. Many Guysborough Liberals were glad, while local Conservatives vowed vengeance. A participant remembered: "With a good supply of old cans and torches, we marched through the streets and stopped at the corner of Dog Lane and Front Street, and it is questionable if there was any more excitement in Gloucester when the *Horton* arrived than there was in Guysborough that night…" The crowd serenaded Torrey and his Conservative friends until "they wished they never seen the *Horton*."

In 1873, much of the Western world fell into an economic depression that lasted until the turn of the twentieth century. In Nova Scotia, where the promise of the economic advantages of political union was put on temporary hold, political disaffection smouldered under the surface of grudging acceptance. Six years after Confederation, the dominant topic of concern in Guysborough was not political, but rather the "August Gale" of 1873. This storm, which made the gale of 1811 seem almost mild by comparison, began on Sunday, August 24, 1873. H. C. Hart, likely a witness, reported that by Sunday evening it was too stormy to attend church services. Overnight, the fury of the storm increased and the "Houses shivered and rocked, so that one was almost afraid to remain indoors, but it was impossible to stand or walk outside…it was an appalling night! Never to be forgotten by those who heard and felt it all." Those with insecure property or vessels in the harbour were forced to crawl, lantern in hand, to check on their losses. At dawn the winds reduced to a mere heavy gale, and the extent of the destruction was proven to be extensive, the Miller's Cove Bridge swept away and part of the Lower Harbour Road washed out. The destruction was such that the man-made topography of the village was changed forever, as many of the wharves and buildings were not replaced. Despite its different face, Guysborough remained the shire town and the chief trading centre for business and supply for an area composed of numerous smaller, outlying communities. It contained professionals like doctors and lawyers; tradespeople like shoemakers, milliners, millers, tailors, blacksmiths, carpenters and ship-builders; businesses such as grist, carding and saw mills, and a tannery; and the myriad of tradesmen and workers demanded by local industry.

Trade with the outside world was conducted by horse and wagon or by sea. Local merchants still conducted a good portion of their business by barter, trading for the surplus products of the farm and ocean. They dealt with scores of families from up and down the shore, as well as those within the village itself. One must be careful not to paint a picture that suggests an idyllic past. Economically, times were tough, prompting numbers of young people or whole families seeking financial security to relocate to the manufacturing centres and gold camps of Nova Scotia or often the United States.

Despite the genteel crust of Guysborough's society and the labours of organizations like the local temperance society, there was a considerable amount of drunkenness among the young men in the seaport town, especially among those who spent the summer at sea and returned home for the winter. Liquor was readily available to those in the know. Fisticuffs were relatively common, and general brawls or melees were not unknown.

The completion of the Intercolonial Railway's link to Sydney in 1891 brought that town into the North American grid of rail and trade. Reid further notes that the industrial output of Nova Scotia increased by sixty percent in the 1880s, and that "the developments of the decade opened up an enticing vision" of prospects for the future. It should not be supposed that the business and commercial leaders in Guysborough did not share this "enticing vision." For example, a meeting was held at the courthouse in January 1877 to "consider the subject of the Eastern Extension Railway, and the duty of Guysborough in connection therewith." The meeting determined, in concert with officials of the neighbouring township of St. Mary's, to send delegates to Halifax to attempt to convince railway officials and government to use a Guysborough County route. A survey for a Guysborough railway line was undertaken, but the arguments were of no avail as the northern Antigonish County line to Sydney was confirmed. Despite this failure, as early as 1890 the Guysborough Municipal Council expressed its willingness to grant twenty years of tax relief to a proposed railway connecting a Guysborough County port to Sunnybrae, Pictou County.

Thereafter, there were various outbreaks of "Railway rumore [sic]" over the years. Construction actually began under a federal government sponsored effort in the late 1920s, but halted in 1930 with a change of government and the onset of the Great Depression. Today the roadbed of the Guysborough Railway forms part of the Trans Canada Trail, and concrete abutments stand in mute testimony to the failed best efforts of local businessmen and politicians. However, the seven miles of track that existed in 1913 continued to be of importance to Guysborough; the 1882 railhead at Mulgrave, Guysborough County, became the destination of the regular packet boats from Guysborough, as well as for the cargoes of fresh fish bound for North American markets. There was also a major realignment of roads from Guysborough to take advantage of the railway station later established at Monastery, Antigonish County.

Having "vision" alone was not enough to promote growth in the community, and the business prospects of other areas did not accrue to Guysborough as the shire town, or to the municipal unit it headed. Indeed, many of the mainstays of the local economy deteriorated, including those that traditionally sustained the community. The decline of the local fishery, the end of the shipbuilding industry in the 1880s and 1890s, and the out-

GUYSBORO, N.S., 1872

Above is a somewhat stylized picture of Guysborough, as it appeared in the *Canadian Illustrated News* on January 13, 1872. While the hills behind the town have been enlarged by this illustrator, the village itself is recognizable. The caption misled the reader by adding an extra zero to the number of residents, but it correctly pointed to its history and economy as a "flourishing seaport town."

migration of workers and their families, all left the local economy caught in the doldrums. In Guysborough, as elsewhere, economic plight found political expression. In the 1880s the voters of the county stood with Premier W.S. Fielding's, albeit temporary, stand on Nova Scotia's secession from Canada. In the election of 1886 many voted for the repeal of the British North America Act and the creation of a union of the Maritime Provinces separate from the rest of the Dominion of Canada. While the results were consistent with the vote of twenty years earlier, the consequences were also similar, as little action resulted. Nonetheless, it gave the people of Guysborough, and the province, an opportunity to express their displeasure with Canada. Other events were also of concern and interest to the people of Guysborough. The turn of the twentieth century saw the emergence of a movement often referred to as the "social gospel," which demanded the improvement of life in this world, and not just the promise of salvation in the next. Christianity did not become less apostolic, but it added new responsibilities to the labours of its missionaries. On September 16, 1883, the Methodist Women's Missionary Society was organized in Guysborough to support foreign and domestic missions, inspiring various sons and daughters of Guysborough to become missionaries.

The construction of the Guysborough Academy brought further changes for young people. The Academy housed classrooms accommodating up to grade eleven, a science laboratory, and a domestic science room intended to prepare young women for what most argued was their truest destiny—as wives and mothers. Many women, however, were determined to postpone or avoid that destiny. Some trained at the Normal School in Truro or obtained a local license, and taught in the classrooms of the little one-room schools that dotted the county. Some became nurses, and still others took the train to New England to pursue employment opportunities—either as domestics, or in the growing industrial economy of the "Boston States." While some of these young women returned to their native area, the continued absence of others was only broken by fond letters or the occasional visit home. Women also worked locally for some of the mercantile and commercial businesses or, after 1894, for the new local newspaper, the Guysborough Gazette. The Gazette's owner and editor, H. Davidson, maintained his business until about 1908, when it was closed. Apparently, when Davidson was told that Guysborough was "laid out" for a city he responded, "Yes, but it was never buried." Perhaps made only partly in jest, this response is likely a good description of Guysborough in the worst of troubled times—it has simply refused to be buried!

A change in centuries generally brings little immediate alteration in the day-to-day affairs of the community, and this was certainly the case in Guysborough. The 1880s and 1890s had been difficult for much of rural Nova Scotia. The promised advantages of Prime Minister Sir John A. Macdonald's National Policy had brought industrialization to some parts of the province, but out-migration and internal-migration continued to strip population from the rest. While the completion of the Intercolonial Railway to Port Mulgrave had opened a market for fresh fish, it also carried more people and business away from Guysborough. More and more local merchants became shopkeepers selling goods to the local people, but no longer engaging in the import and export trade of their predecessors. As the students of the Academy later reported, the "fortunes of the town had always depended upon the sea and with the decline of fishing, shipbuilding, and trade, Guysborough languished."

The village itself, however, continued in its role as the government and business centre for the district. It had the largest, newest school, and many a student from the rural one-room common schools came to town to further their studies at the Guysborough Academy.

MINERS FROM THE FOREST HILL MINES, C.1890S

The discovery of gold in 1860s in the Sherbrooke area contributed to the growth of that entire district. Closer to Guysborough, gold was discovered by Samuel D. Hudson in June 1893 at Forest Hill, and by 1896 a mining town had been carved out of the wilderness. It had three gold stamp mills, stores, a school house and a population between two and three hundred. By 1950 the village was deserted, but during its heyday it meant business for the mercantile houses and government officials in its shire town.

Military tensions were growing in the Western world, and the difficult times in Guysborough were partly relieved by the outbreak of World War One. Ian McKay points out that the wartime economic upturn spread across the economy. He wrote: "Wartime prosperity extended beyond manufacturing: the fisheries were more active than they had been for years; farmers throve on a higher demand for their products and on higher prices; lumbermen exploited new market possibilities, such as supplying British collieries with the pit props they could no longer obtain in Europe. There even seemed to be new hope for wooden shipbuilding."

The increased prosperity no doubt raised people's spirits, but the greatest effect of the war was the outpouring of patriotic fever that accompanied it. By 1918, McKay reports, "approximately 30,500 Nova Scotia men, 37 percent of the male population between eighteen and forty-five, had enrolled for service, with an additional 7,000 employed in home defense." The people of Guysborough were not remiss in their duty, and many young men went overseas to fight for King and Country, soon amassing a roll of war dead in every church in the community. Some urban women were engaged as white feather vigilantes in support of the war effort, seeking shirkers—men who avoided military service—to whom they awarded the white feather of cowardice. In the words of the Halifax Herald, commonly read in Guysborough, "The Duty of Every Nova Scotia Woman, Every Nova Scotia Girl Today Is to See that Men Folk Fight or Farm: Women Must Show the Way to Loafers, Funkers, and Pink Tea Tango Boys." The political activity of Guysborough women had traditionally been in the vanguard of the Temperance Movement, which also reached its zenith in World War One, but this was not the only issue that stirred them to action. They were also active in support of the war-cause; they rolled bandages, and knitted endless numbers of socks and underwear for soldiers. With the Guysborough Municipal Council, the women financially supported the Canadian Patriotic Fund. They mourned the lost, or welcomed their sons and husbands home to Guysborough.

Women were equally concerned with the place and political power of their gender. Along with many men, they signed suffrage petitions demanding the vote for women. The March 12, 1918 petition to the Legislative Assembly of Nova Scotia called upon the Legislature to grant "the provincial franchise to women upon the same terms as those upon which is granted to men." Participants included 497 residents of Guysborough County and 67 Guysborough women and men from all backgrounds and occupations: the bank manager, jeweller, merchants, clerks, teachers, milliners, clergy, stenographers, councillors, lawyers, medical doctor, assistant post mistress, commercial travellers, hotel keepers, and housewives. This support for a movement both province- and nation-wide brought results when, in that same year of 1918, women were granted full political rights in Nova Scotia, rights that were also recognized on the federal level.

The economic promise of the war years turned to dust and ashes in the 1920s. John G. Reid contends that the Great Depression, which marked the 1930s in much of the Western world began "in the Maritimes…in the summer of 1920 and lasted for a full generation." The Depression was fought tenaciously, but new international competition, world trade disruptions, and later national protectionism meant that the sales of even the natural products of land, sea, and forest were threatened. The export of salt fish showed signs of depletion, but the decline was offset for a time "by increased output of fresh and frozen fish for the New England market." This helped to cushion the blow to Guysborough, as did the Sonora Timber Company's trade in pulp wood. The Company provided sales for woodlot owners and employment to company woods crews and stevedores in Guysborough, Sherbrooke, and elsewhere, at ten cents an hour in a ten hour day, loading pulpwood for export to the United States. The Company went bankrupt in 1932, however, and even that employment was denied.

E. R. Forbes explained the depths of the financial situation. "After decades of rural depopulation, Guysborough County, for example, had no reserves with which to cushion the disruption of its lumbering and fishing industries. Unable to collect more than a third of its taxes and denied bank credit, it was virtually bankrupt by June of 1931." Caught in such a financial bind and nonetheless responsible for social assistance, the poorest areas, like Guysborough County, "might make available a dollar per person to several hundred unemployed one month and give them nothing the next." By the mid to late 1930s some additional road work was available to those who were known to have supported the victorious political party as, in 1936, the Guysborough Municipal Council approved the location of Route 4 between the railhead at Monastery and Port Mulgrave. Its other attempt to improve transportation in the 1930s failed, despite Council's petition to the federal government for an airport in the municipality. Guysborough, a supply centre and the seat of local government, weathered these times as best it could. A local troop of the Boy Scouts was created in 1923, and other church and fraternal organizations were maintained. Like the rest of the province after 1921, Guysborough was officially "dry," implementing the popular social forces of temperance and later prohibition. The liquor trade was restored under government regulation in Nova Scotia in 1929. Even during the years of local prohibition, "rum running to the United States was a lucrative business in many coastal areas of the Maritimes," as fishermen and others augmented their income until the liquor trade was also resumed in the United States.

The economic problems of the community unfortunately extended to the schools. In 1929, its new Board of Trustees found that Guysborough School Section, No.1, the seat of Guysborough Academy (the high school of the district) was in financial ruin. Laurier Grant

Guysboro, Nova Scotia.

GUYSBOROUGH CIRCA 1900

reported that its "teachers had not been paid their quarterly salary at the end of June and [the] school section was virtually bankrupt. There were unpaid school taxes totalling over $10,000.00." By squeezing every cent at least twice, the three trustees imposed every economy, and by 1942 "had most of the debts paid off and the unpaid taxes reduced to a few hundred dollars." This was a remarkable feat in the midst of the most difficult of economic times.

Though labouring under the economic depression of the 1920s and 1930s, Guysborough managed a dramatic step toward modernization. The county did not have rural electric service until the 1940s and 1950s, but a small group of people made plans in 1927 to provide electric light to the shire town of about three hundred and fifty residences. In that year a "syndicate of small time entrepreneurs decided to form a joint stock company…to supply a minimum of electric light and power to the town each day from one hour before sunset to one hour after sunrise." The Guysboro Heat, Light and Power Co. was born, and its officers moved quickly to purchase land, erect a building, and obtain the equipment necessary to produce electricity. For under three dollars a month each, about eighty customers were supplied with electricity, though the hours of availability were limited. When some households purchased electric washing machines, the company agreed to "remain in operation until twelve noon on Monday of each week, for the convenience of housewives, and others with laundry appliances."

Though the Stock Market crash in 1929 sent most stock prices dramatically downward, the stocks of the Guysborough Heat, Light and Power Co. actually increased in value. In 1929, the company began a two-year experiment to provide street lights to the community. In 1939, after twelve years of service, the company's assets were sold to the Nova Scotia Power Commission at a profit to its shareholders.

Immersed in the economic and social difficulties at home, the people of Guysborough and their fellows across the Maritimes almost welcomed the outbreak of war in September 1939. Employment rates rose and a degree of optimism returned—albeit an optimism dampened by new concerns about sons and daughters serving in the military. World War Two, like the first, saw the little community on Chedabucto Bay participate fully in the war effort. Both men and women served in the armed forces and became part of the military reserve, one platoon of which was stationed at Guysborough. They worked in war industries and participated in all the drives, rationing, Red Cross activities, fund raising, and whatever else needed to be done to support the war machine. Locals cheered the victory of 1945 and their country's part in it; once again they mourned their lost and welcomed their troops home.

The Guysborough Memorial Hospital celebrated its official opening in the 1940s, just in time to service the demand brought on by the baby boom of the 1940s and 1950s. The increased birth rate led to a need for modern education facilities. When Guysborough Municipal High School was opened in 1960, many rural schools were closed, and for the first time a fleet of buses carried students into Guysborough daily.

The Guysborough of the 1940s and 1950s was not physically unlike the Guysborough of 1900, or indeed the Guysborough of today. The shape of the streets is still the same and, though replaced or augmented by new buildings, plenty of the old buildings and ancient trees still grace the community. As the Guysboro Heat, Light and Power Co. intended, street lights still offers comfort to late-night walkers, though more in the style of the kerosene lamps of the turn of the last century. The traditional downtown commercial centre of the village has been transplanted to the shopping mall, but many of the buildings themselves remain and are used commercially. The waterfront, which once rang with the shouts of stevedores and sailors, is now a marina that accommodates both leisurely and cultural pursuits. It remains a vibrant part of the community. As harbours have traditionally been in this province, the community remains the educational, administrative, and commercial supply centre of its small world. The schools, government offices, and retail outlets still offer a buffer of economic protection to the community, as they have since the 1780s—and Guysborough still refuses to be buried.

During its several hundred years of life, Guysborough has been something of an enigma. While the Guysborough area was one of the first reported European landfalls on the mainland of North America, it is only recently that this has been marked for public information. While this area played a significant role in the French period of Nova Scotia's history, its prominence has been more commonly denied than celebrated. Populated with military and proven in its loyalty, it has never celebrated its military heritage. Settled by a group with an educated leadership, and always a centre of schooling, it has never drawn attention to itself as either a scholarly or schooled community. An historical centre of business and commerce, Guysborough's activity in shipbuilding and export trade could also be better known.

Over one hundred and fifty years ago, Joseph Howe, while admitting that he had only previously associated Guysborough with fish, was fulsome in praise of the beauty of the community. Today, while the people of Guysborough may realize the beauty of their physical environment, here again they have been overly modest in its celebration. Likewise, while the community has always contained a population with English, Irish, Scottish, German, Acadian, African Nova Scotian, Mi'kmaq, Russian, and other representation, Guysborough has drawn little attention to its racial and cultural diversity.

Outsiders might wonder how such a community continues to exist, and why it holds the heartstrings of many of its expatriate sons and daughters who still consider it their home. While the source of attachment to the place is likely as varied as the people who feel the sentiment, it must go beyond the natural beauty of Guysborough, snugly located on the bank of the estuary of the Milford Haven River that is Guysborough Harbour. It must also be more than friends or even families left behind, because so many of every generation have gone. It is more than the services provided in the community, or nostalgia for child-hood. Whatever makes Guysborough feel like home to so many is both difficult to define and impossible to measure. For many the pull they have toward this town is as real as the moonlight reflected on the harbour, the evening breeze, the curl of fog off the coast, the first glimpse of red leaves in the fall, the sun's heat on a summer afternoon, or a casual wave from someone not surprised to see you home.

Chapter 1

The Shire Town

STREET VIEW OF JAIL, COURTHOUSE AND REGISTRAR OF DEEDS, 1937

As the capital of its political district, Guysborough was home to the local, provincial, and later federal government offices. It offered other major services, such as the Guysborough Academy, the larger churches, the hospital, the central post office and customs office, and other vestiges of officialdom.

THE GUYSBOROUGH COURTHOUSE, CONSTRUCTED 1843

The courthouse was constructed by Elisha Randall, a builder from nearby Bayfield. The building is unusual in its Gothic style, which was more commonly found in churches. Originally, the courthouse also had a belfry, which enhanced further its resemblance to a church.

Many of the Loyalists were well-schooled in local politics and township government, and the pioneer families made provision for local government within a year of their arrival at Guysborough. On October 11, 1785, the Court of General Sessions of the Peace, which bore the double responsibility of being the governing body and the local court of justice, met for the first time. The Sessions heard a case of assault and battery, appointed town and county officials, arranged for "licenses to sell Spirituous Liquors" and adjourned until May 1786. At that next meeting of the Sessions, in their first money vote, they agreed to spend eighty pounds to build a courthouse and jail and two pounds to provide authorities with "Public Stocks and Bolts and Shackles." The jail, which could have been made of logs, seems to have been built first. It was erected at the head of Miller's Cove and was soon put to use. The constables were admonished to "exert themselves on the Lords Day in frequenting the Public Houses" and charging "all such persons as shall be found Drinking and Rioting therein in Time of Divine Service."

While most crimes were no doubt minor offences, even these earned stiff penalties. More than one man, and some women, were sentenced, as the court record reads, to "receive on his naked Back, Thirty Nine Stripes, at the Public Whipping post" in Guysborough. This sentence was brought down on one unfortunate for having stolen a hoe and, to add insult to obvious injury, the court deemed him "an Idle, Lazy, Vagabond," ordering that he "be bound out to some good Master, to pay for all costs and charges attending this prosecution."

In 1793 the Sessions voted one hundred pounds to build a courthouse and a new jail in one building, also located at the head of Miller's Cove. It was there that Lee, the cooper, was tried for murder which he committed "by the use of a certain stone of no value." Judge Monk came from Halifax to hear the case, and Lee, "not having the fear of God before his eyes but being moved and seduced by the instigation of the devil," was sentenced to be hanged. According to Hart, he "suffered the extreme penalty of the law from an upper window of the Court House."

By 1818, the Sessions determined that the building should be replaced, and a new building was erected on Church Street, housing court rooms, jail, and the keeper's quarters. Within twenty years, this arrangement was no longer considered adequate, and the building was sold in 1843 to the "Town Hall Company," which "hauled it up the road with oxen" to another site. The new courthouse and jail were completed in 1843, this time as two distinct buildings. The cells on the first floor of the jail were for common felons, while those on the second floor were reserved for women and debtors. A high board fence enclosed an exercise yard for the prisoners, but neither cells nor fence were guaranteed to keep certain felons in custody. Although the first jailkeeper in Guysborough was charged with aiding the escape of some prisoners, and another lost his liquor licence when his salary was increased, neither vigilance nor sobriety always sufficed. On one occasion a prisoner from Antigonish, held for some misdemeanour, was broken out of jail by his indignant friends. They paraded defiantly around town in horse drawn wagons, playing the bagpipes, before decamping and returning home. Some prisoners simply climbed over the fence in the light of day and ran away, but others planned their escapes more carefully. Most were content to stay and serve their time and walk away with no one in pursuit. Law and order were maintained by locally appointed constables until 1932, when a detachment of the Royal Canadian Mounted Police was opened in Guysborough.

The new courthouse was equipped with a judge's bench, witness box, space for the grand and petite jury, and all the other paraphernalia considered necessary. These buildings were suitably cared for and served the people of the Guysborough District for over one hundred and forty years before they were replaced. The jail is gone, but the courthouse has been preserved and now serves the community as the local museum. Over its life time, it witnessed many of the marked events of the history of the community. Political decisions were made here, trials conducted and sentences delivered, exhibitions held, ballots cast in dozens of elections, visiting dignitaries greeted, and lives offered in war time. The courthouse was such a long-standing physical representation of law and justice that much credit should be given to the local historical society for undertaking the Herculean task of preserving it for posterity. Today, neither courthouse nor jail exists in Guysborough. While the current Municipal Building contained both facilities, they were closed by provincial authorities after more than two hundred and ten years of service in the shire town.

THE MERCHANTS' BANK (LATER THE ROYAL BANK) ON MAIN STREET, c.1890

During the early years of settlement in Guysborough, any cash money that individuals or businesses possessed was privately secured or held in a merchant's safe. This arrangement became inconvenient as the economy became increasingly cash driven. The situation was rectified on September 18, 1882, when a branch or agency of the Merchants Bank of Halifax opened its doors to clients in Guysborough. Located in the former general store of the Hon. C.M. Francheville, MLC, the first local manager or agent was Henry Marshall Jost. The Merchants Bank itself had been founded in Halifax in 1864 by local merchants (hence its name), and it received its federal charter in 1869. In the late 1880s, it moved its headquarters to Montreal, and changed its name in 1901 to the Royal Bank of Canada. Just as the early managers were local people, so too were many of the employees. In 1912 junior clerks were hired with a grade seven to ten education and paid a starting salary of two hundred dollars per year.

Major crime was uncommon in Guysborough, but still the bank supplied each of its tellers with a .38 calibre revolver, insisting that the guns be displayed on the desk in plain view during banking hours. This implied threat may be the reason that the most significant attempted robbery took place at night. On the morning of March 7, 1913, one of the junior clerks arrived early to perform the janitorial services demanded of his rank, and found that an attempt had been made to crack the seven foot high combination book and cash safe. The yeggman had broken off the combination dial, inserted a charge of nitroglycerine, took cover, and blew off the double safe doors. The charge also blew out all the doors and windows on the main floor, ejecting one of the twenty-pound hinges of the safe all the way to the field across the street from the bank. The would-be robbers failed to gain access to the inner cash compartment, however, which was doubly protected by a second two-inch steel door and a time lock. Frustrated by the failed effort, they escaped. While the investigating Royal Canadian Mounted Police detective was confident that he knew the identities of the villains, he was unable to obtain sufficient evidence for an arrest. Bank security was increased until a new safe could be installed; the three clerks were supplied with .32 calibre automatic pistols, and required to remain on guard at night. Beds were installed for them on the second floor.

The attic of the bank was used on other occasions as well. Fred Buckley remembered a night that occurred around 1922. Some of the boys working at the bank were in the attic playing cards, "carrying on," and upset the stove. A couple of them scrambled to scoop up the scattered hot coals, while another ran to the Buckley home with a bucket for water. However, on arrival he was informed that they had just tuned in WBZ on Walter Buckley's first radio. The clerk became so interested to hear the American station that he forgot his mission and went upstairs to join those listening. Suddenly he recalled what he had come for and exclaimed, "Oh, I forgot I came to get a bucket of water; the bank's on fire!" And off he dashed.

In "Recollections," Laurier Grant recounts memories of his four-year term as a junior clerk in Guysborough: the pre-1935 Bank of Canada bank notes from the various chartered banks; the bank manager spending a full day countersigning the Royal Bank notes to make them legal tender; the gold coins; the twenty-five cent notes or shin plasters; and the few 1882 four-dollar bills that were still in circulation. He spent his busiest day as a teller when the Fenian Raid Bounty of one hundred dollars was paid to veterans of seventy or more years of age. The old bank building still stands, although it has since served other uses. In 1977, after ninety-four years of business at that site, the Bank moved into new quarters.

Ship owners, merchants, and private citizens alike depended on the Royal Mail to enable communication with the outside world. Prior to the establishment of a post office, letters were sent to Antigonish, the distribution point for the eastern sections of the province. When a decent number had accumulated, the postmaster would bundle them up and forward them to Guysborough in the trust of Robert M. Cutler. Cutler, in turn, would hold them at his father's home at Cutler's Cove for distribution to the proper recipients.

In 1825 a postal way office was established in Guysborough; Cutler served as Postmaster. In 1832, the office was moved from Cutler's Cove to the lower part of the town, which had become the chief business centre. There it fell under the direction of Edward Irish Cunningham. In 1832, Cunningham established his own general store, and the postal way office was "given unto his care. In 1841, the facility was officially made a post office, and Cunningham was responsible for its management for fifty-five years.

The new post office, a major construction project in Guysborough at the turn of the century, was built by contractor E. F. Munroe of Westville. Its design was the responsibility of the Chief Architects' branch of the federal Department of Public Works under David Ewart (1897–1914). The Canadian government was determined to raise its profile in towns and cities across the country, and Public Works was responsible for the creation of a recognizable Dominion image of architecture. The Guysborough building was one of some eighty combined post office and customs office structures which were often among the most distinguished buildings in their communities. The Guysborough office served as the collection and distribution point for over thirty dependent offices, and for over one hundred years the people of Guysborough have met at the post office to receive and send mail. The clock in the tower has tolled the hours faithfully since W. H. Buckley installed it in 1910.

Guysboro, N.S. 1891. WH. Photo.

THE GUYSBOROUGH ACADEMY OF THE 1860s, 1891

As the shire town of the county, Guysborough was the local centre of higher education. Common schools dotted the countryside by 1878, and the Academy at Guysborough provided students from these schools with access to the senior grades necessary for entry to university or the Normal School in Truro. Patrick Patton is generally credited with being one of the first school masters in the community. He was likely near his twentieth year of service when, in the famous gale of 1811, he maintained regular school hours, although "when the hour for dismission came the children had to crawl home, as none was able to stand before the fury of the tempest."

The third grammar school in the province, which offered higher grades (although "grades" as such did not become common until the 1880s), had been established in Guysborough under provincial legislation in 1811, and a new school house was built by 1814. The need for larger and more modern facilities was evident by 1843, when the town hall was pressed into service as a school room. By the 1860s, the one hundred and fifty students in "constant attendance" occupied several buildings in the community as they waited for the Academy building to be completed. Inspector Samuel R. Russell, a ship-wrecked native of England who had been teaching in the area since the 1830s, was pleased to report in 1866 that the "Guysborough Academy, measuring 75 by 33 feet, with sixteen foot posts, and a playground of one acre, is now not only finished and supplied with all necessary outbuildings, but furnished in all three departments with patent desks and seats, and is at this time in full operation with a staff of two male and one female teachers, and an attendance of at least 150 pupils…" The new school was the pride of the village and the community supported it accordingly. In 1874, the students "held a bazaar and concert in August, when a tasteful collection of articles of their own work was offered for sale. The proceeds purchased a bell and clock for the Academy."

The needs of the community soon exceeded the 1866 Academy's capabilities, and a new Academy was built in 1895. Local contractor George Y. Grant agreed to construct the building, providing all material and labour, for $1,800. The late James Skinner related how his father Nathanial (Nate) contracted to dig the basement for the building. After paying for the use of horses and scoops and hand labour, he had only one dollar left for himself. The local school inspector, W. MacIsaac, commented in his 1895 report to the Superintendent of Education that the "new academy in Guysboro, which has been erected during this year, is an excellent specimen of the ideal school building." He complimented its "beautiful position near the site of the old academy" and noted that it was "an ornament to the town and a lasting testimony of the public spirit and generosity of the citizens." This nicely proportioned building represented the best the community could offer. It had four major classrooms that housed three grades to a room, a domestic science room, and a laboratory. The old bell in the copula called students to their studies for over ninety years. The first bell warned, the second bell insisted, but on occasion there were a few minutes' reprieve. If the heroic senior boy entrusted with ringing the bell accidentally turned it upside down, he had to climb into the belfry to right the bell before it could peal out its final summons. The school grounds were active with games of ball, hopscotch, volleyball, soccer, and races during recess, dinner hour, and after school. They were also the site of School Field Days, when students from the surrounding rural school houses would come into town for the day.

GUYSBOROUGH MUNICIPAL HIGH SCHOOL, c.1965

The 1895 Academy building was eventually replaced by Guysborough Municipal High School which opened on May 17, 1961. The school year of 1960–1961 was much like that of 1865–1866, when each empty space in the village was converted to a classroom until the new school building could be occupied. Guysborough Academy was restored in 1978, and used for office space and storage until it was destroyed by fire on August 13, 1980. Guysborough Municipal High School is also gone, having fallen to wreckers' hammers in January 2001, when it was replaced by yet another Guysborough Academy. This new building will serve the community into the foreseeable future.

School Field Day
Guysborough N.S. 1933

SCHOOL FIELD DAY AT GUYSBOROUGH ACADEMY, 1933

School Field Days, like this one in 1933, brought the students of the local schools into town to the Academy where they would each present a program. Fine weather and an appreciative audience of parents were two elements necessary for a successful day. The upstretched arms of the man directly in front of the students from the South Interval School seem to suggest that they are about to present a song. For years, the Royal Bank of Canada trophy was awarded to the most successful school at the School Field Day.

THE ROYAL BANK TROPHY, 1930s

This trophy, donated by the Royal Bank of Canada, was awarded to the school that earned the highest average points at the Guysborough County School Fairs. The shields on its bottom recognized the winning school. The trophy is held in the collection of the Old Court House Museum.

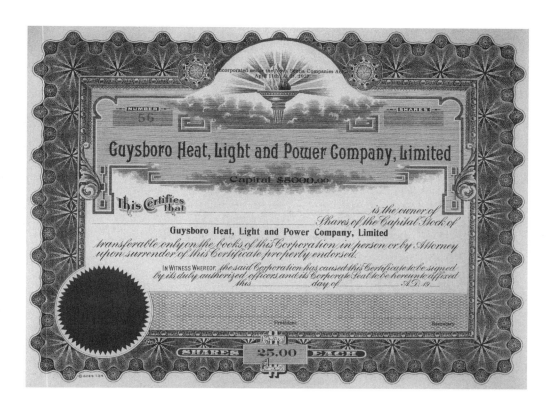

STOCK CERTIFICATE FOR THE GUYSBORO HEAT, LIGHT AND POWER COMPANY, EST. 1927

In the 1920s, Guysborough residents heated their homes and cooked with coal or wood, used kerosene lamps and candles for light, and listened to battery powered radios. While much of rural Guysborough County had to wait until the 1950s for electricity, it was made available to the village in 1927. A small group of local entrepreneurs created a joint stock company in the spring of that year, naming it the Guysboro Heat, Light and Power Company. With the approval of the provincial Board of Commissioners of Public Utilities, the new company moved quickly to purchase a lot of land near the shore (close to what is now the government wharf), to construct a building, and to acquire a diesel motor and a direct current generator. Within seven months the plant was operating near capacity, and its directors moved to reduce the rate to their subscribers. In 1928, due to public demand, additional equipment was procured and increased and better service provided to the company's eighty customers. Originally, the company provided power each day from one hour before sunset to one hour after sunrise. However, as customers acquired additional electrical appliances and altered their motors from alternating to direct current, the plant remained "in operation until twelve noon on Monday of each week, for the convenience of housewives, and others with laundry appliances." Despite the stock market crash of 1929 and the onset of the Great Depression of the 1930s, the Guysboro Heat, Light and Power Co. remained financially solid and its shares retained their value. The company was able to reduce charges to its customers and to invest its surpluses, resulting in a 1934 purchase of a five-hundred-dollar debenture of Guysborough School Section No. 1.

From 1929 to 1931 the company maintained a system of up to twenty-five low wattage street lights, which Fred Buckley said looked like a string of fireflies. Service was discontinued, however, as the company was not able to collect enough to cover full maintenance costs. In 1938, faced by the demands of its customers and the expectations of system upgrades, the directors agreed to consider selling the company to the Nova Scotia Power Commission. Offers and counter-offers were exchanged in 1939, and the assets of the Guysborough Heat, Light and Power Co. were sold to the Nova Scotia Power Commission on July 31st of that year, although a shell company was maintained to satisfy the requirements of the H. M. Jost estate.

The Commission moved to build a water-powered plant at Dickey's Brook, supported by the linkage of a network of lakes, and the construction of a tower and flume to drive the turbines. This plant provided alternating current electric power to both the village and an ever-growing rural area.

GUYSBOROUGH'S FIRST PUMPER (1912)

Communities built of wood must be wary of fire. Guysborough's earliest pioneers remembered the destruction of their homes in today's Port Mouton, prior to their move to the estuary of Milford Haven. For more than a century of Guysborough's existence, when fire threatened the residents' flues, houses, and businesses, it had to be handled as quickly as possible by a handful of neighbours and a bucket brigade. When a local blacksmith shop burned down, the community recognized its good fortune that the wind was blowing out over the harbour and spared other buildings from catching fire. Those threats prompted the community to purchase a pump in 1912, and other fire fighting equipment was obtained in 1925 by voluntary subscription and supported by a grant of thirty dollars from the Municipal Council. The Council explained that their contribution was to protect the jail, courthouse, and Registry of Deeds buildings in Guysborough.

The 1912 rocker bar pump was operated by six to eight men and equipped with a 1/2-inch hose and a 3/8 inch nozzle. The pump and the men were tested in December 1927 when Jost's Store caught fire. The building, standing three stories in front and four in the back, stood in a cluster of businesses, warehouses, and residences on Lower Main Street, and was filled with combustibles including paint, kerosene, and linseed oil. The firefighters' main objective was to prevent the fire from spreading to other buildings. The leather valves in the pump dried out and would not draw, so the pump itself was immersed in the harbour and men took turns standing in the cold December water and pumped to save Main Street. The man holding the nozzle faced so much heat that the others had to throw buckets of water on him as he worked to save the small house next to the store. Eventually, he was given a big metal sign that had been torn off the store's gasoline pump and he found some relief in standing behind it while he poured water on the house. The store was lost, but the houses were saved and the fire was contained. Later, three small forest-fire pumps of about five-horse power each were purchased for firefighting. However, the available equipment was no match for big fires like the one that destroyed the Masonic Hall in 1933. The community was prompted to buy its first self-contained fire truck and reorganize the fire department in 1954, after a child died in a house fire.

Twelve members of the Guysborough Fire Department in front of Truck #2. The fire truck, the department's first self-contained ladder truck, had an on-board water tank and equipment lockers. The two men in the back are Mike Long and Joseph Leet. In front, from left to right, are: Charlie Dort, Walter MacDonald, Lindsay Jones, Ralph Young, Fire Chief Clyde Jones, Leland Williams, Laurier Andrews, Jack Brody, Bernard Worth, and an unidentified man. Pumper #1 was a Ford Model "A", converted to cut firewood to length and pump water. Some will remember the "Ladder House" beside the Glebe, the fire wells, ladders, and other equipment. The reorganized volunteer fire department obtained a freight warehouse from Harts Wharf in the mid-1950s and moved it to Main Street. It served as the Fire Hall for a number of years. Today a new fire hall contains the modern equipment of an active volunteer fire department.

THE
CHEDABUCTO
HALL OF THE
SONS OF
TEMPERANCE,
QUEEN STREET,
C.1910

The building that served several generations as the Masonic Hall was originally constructed to be a Presbyterian church. It was named for an eccentric
local farmer who willed property, the proceeds of which funded the church's
construction. But the Presbyterian community was not large enough to sus-
tain itself, and sold the building in 1859 to the local division of the Sons of
Temperance, who moved it so its end turned to Queen Street. They named
it Chedabucto Hall. As the largest hall in the community until the 1960s, it
remained a centre for gatherings of many kinds: political meetings, dances,
music festivals, plays, suppers, school concerts, strawberry festivals, military
recruitment, and of course for the temperance meetings.

After their building burned down in 1933, the Masons purchased
Chedabucto Hall and altered the building for their own purposes. Thereafter,
the new second floor was reserved for Masonic use, and the first floor hall for
the community. The premier performance of every play of the local Mulgrave
Road Theatre Company is still presented in the first floor playhouse. In this
picture, Chedabucto Hall's ecclesiastical windows face the camera. The outline
of these windows was still clearly evident the last time the building was shin-
gled. The two large houses on the right were the homes of Burton and George
Jost, Hillside and Rosebank respectively.

THE METHODIST SUNDAY SCHOOL PICNIC, 1914

Sunday school was an important part of children's lives in Guysborough, and each of the local churches eventually organized a Sunday School for the religious education of their young people. The very first was created by Charlotte Newton in 1822. The original minute book reveals that instruction began with spellings at 8 A.M. followed by the usual Sunday School lessons. When the session ended, the students were marched by their teachers to church. The first Sunday School's library was stocked with contributions from townspeople and others, providing the students with copies of *Bromley's Catechism* and other worthy books.

The individual religious communities in Guysborough each established their own denominational Sunday schools. Hilda Cox remembered attending the Methodist Sunday school, which had its own building constructed in 1876. She first attended sessions of the Mission Band in a baby carriage, as her mother was in charge of it. Once they were able, she and her brothers and sisters walked to Sunday school every week of their youth, as there was no summer recess. There was even a Bible study class for young adults. After the Sunday school classes ended, everyone crossed the corner to church. The Methodist Sunday school building was also used for Friday evening "prayer meetings," and meetings of the Epworth league. A ladies' parlour was added in later days, while the assembly hall continued to be used for Sunday school classes, by the Canadian Girls in Training (CGIT), Explorers, Cubs ,and Scouts. Unnumbered "tea and sales" in support of the work of the church were held in this building.

McIsaac's Hall of St. Ann's Parish, Queen Street, 1940s

McIsaac's Hall was named in honour of Rev. W. B. McIsaac (a.k.a. Father Billy), the parish priest in charge of Guysborough (1928–1950). It was built by the Roman Catholic congregation in 1932 and has been used ever since for church purposes and for a variety of community functions. Picnics were held beside and within it for years, featuring games of chance, food booths, dunk tanks, and all the old attractions for young people. It also housed a boxing club, for which a ring was constructed. Among the featured boxers was young Leslie Borden from nearby Boylston, who went on to hold the Canadian Light Heavyweight title from 1965 to 1968. Borden later fought as a heavyweight, and battled such notables as George Chavalo, Jerry Quarry, and Bill drover, travelling the world from his homebase in Montreal.

Competitions were staged there between local and visiting tug-of-war teams. On one occasion, locals conspired to use an overly long rope, a constricted area, and a mask of bushes to their advantage, hitching the end of the rope to a horse and ensuring their victory. Bingo games were a regular feature, and many young people saw their first movie in McIsaac's Hall. The annual music festival used this facility as well, and it continues to serve as a meeting place for both the congregation and the larger community.

THE
GUYSBOROUGH
RED CROSS
HOSPITAL
(1939–1949)
NEAR THE MILL
BROOK, 1940s

During its lifetime, Guysborough has been fortunate to secure dedicated medical doctors to serve the needs of its residents. The pioneer settlers long praised Dr. Ludovic Joppee, who had come with the 60th Regiment. H. C. Hart comments on the "wonderful stories of his skill in the healing arts" and on his "little pony, Lively, that so often carried him over the rough wood paths" to visit his far-flung patients. For a later generation, Dr. George Buckley became an almost legendary figure, attending to the medical needs of the community by horse or on foot, in gzs the first hospital or "nursing station." Arrangements were made, staff hired, a nurse appointed, and the six-bed facility opened in early 1940. It was one of the first Outpost Hospitals established in Nova Scotia. It was maintained by patient fees, a grant from the Municipality, the untiring voluntary labour of the Committee, and the contributions of the Red Cross branches in many of the surrounding communities.

It is no wonder that hospital personnel changed in time, as the nurse was on call twenty-four hours a day and the pay was low. Laurier Grant noted that the caretaker and his wife resigned around 1940, and were replaced by Jean McKay of Guysborough Interval. Grant writes: "This unusual and remarkable person managed the household during the next several years; her duties consisted of being cook, assisting the nurse in emergencies, helping with the sterilizing, which was done on the kitchen stove, and many other duties including the milking, feeding and caring of two cows." For this she received a few hundred dollars a year and her board, although as Grant points out, "she received some extra compensation by raising a calf which was sold at a good price." The Guysborough Red Cross Hospital continued to function for a number of years with a small, over-worked staff and primitive, inadequate equipment. The members of the committee came to the conclusion that they either had to find suitable facilities or give up the entire effort. Consequently, in February 1946 the committee convened a meeting of citizens who determined that their course was to move forward. A draft of incorporation had already been sent to the Legislative Assembly and a temporary slate of officers was elected.

GUYSBOROUGH MEMORIAL HOSPITAL (1949–1988) AT BELMONT, 1948

It was revealed that Henry Marshall Tory, a former Guysborough resident, had offered his "Belmont Farm" home to serve as the hospital when he was finished with it. He had made provision in his will for the house and land to be turned over to the local hospital organization, and recommended that they draw plans for any necessary external changes so that when the time came, no time would be lost in preparation. A financial campaign was launched at once and an architect was chosen to prepare plans to turn Belmont Farm into a twenty-bed cottage hospital.

On February 6, 1947, Dr. Tory died. His last letter was addressed to the hospital committee, urging them to go ahead on their own. The tenders were called by January 1948, but the committee decided to turn the project over to a local foreman, to hire local workmen, and to be their own general contractors. While this decision added immeasurably to the work of the volunteer committee, it significantly reduced the cost of the project to the community. Guysborough Memorial Hospital was officially opened on November 5, 1949, with ceremonies that attracted about five hundred people. Later extended, the hospital served the needs of the public until 1988 when a new faculty that combined Guysborough Memorial Hospital with the Milford Haven Home for Special Care was constructed.

The Roman Catholic Church has been in Guysborough longer than any other Christian denomination. It dates to the early French period, when the community was under the care of resident priests like Father Martin de Lyonne, and those priests brought in 1686 by merchant Sieur Bergier (although he was a Protestant) to serve his Catholic employees and neighbours.

The modern Roman Catholic Church in Guysborough dates back to the establishment of the parish of St. Ann. Father James Grant was its founding priest and he began the first parochial register on July 9, 1819. The original parish of St. Ann was concentrated at the settlements of the newly arrived Irish immigrants and the more established Acadian communities. Shortly after the parish was established, the first St. Ann's Church was constructed. It was built out of logs about two miles from the present site. A glebe house was built at Guysborough about the same time. A second St. Ann's was built to replace the log structure in the 1840s on the grounds of the third and current parish church. The second St. Ann's witnessed much strife between the local parish priest and his bishop. Johnston records the bishop's arrival in Guysborough to address the issue, and subsequent discovery that he was locked out of the church and "had to have the door forced open and have the sheriff and officers guard the door" while he conducted mass. While no hint is given as to the nature of the disagreement, it was such that "His Lordship lodged not in the Glebe but with a good Presbyterian." The local priest, who had failed to maintain the parochial register, soon found himself elsewhere, after which "all was quiet."

In 1871, the people of St. Ann's Parish established a fund for the construction of a new church. By then the old building was in such need of repair that Father Michael Tomkins wrote: "It was so very shaky that all but the deaf would leave when a storm came up on Sundays." The new structure, only half finished, withstood the fury and destruction of the August Gale of 1873, and one week later, on Sunday, August 31, 1873, Bishop Colin MacKinnon blessed the corner stone. By 1877, the interior was both finished and paid for, and Bishop John Cameron blessed the building on July 22 of that year. In 1880, a new glebe house was also erected. While the glebe has since been replaced, St. Ann's Church continues to serve its congregation.

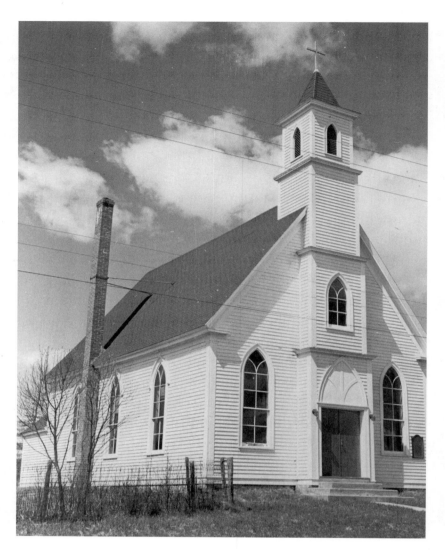

It is likely—though not entirely certain—that the majority of the Loyalists and disbanded military that established Guysborough were adherents of the Church of England. Accordingly, the first Christian church building in the new settlement represented the Church of England. The first clergyman was the Rev. Peter de la Roche, a native of Geneva, Switzerland. He was a missionary cleric of the Society for the Propagation of the Gospel, ordained in 1771 and serving Lunenburg when he made a 1786 trip to Chedabucto on private business. In Guysborough he baptized 144 children, held services, and so impressed people that they applied to the Society for his ministry. Noting that the community had been without a clergyman for two years, the applicants promised to pay his moving expenses and provide him with a house and fuel. The Society agreed, and on July 6, 1787, de la Roche arrived with his family to assume his duties in the parish.

The first Christ Church was built in 1790—on the same site as today's church—with a belfry, small bell, and a three story pulpit, the lower of which was occupied by the clerk who led the responses. It served its congregation until the gale of 1811 blew it down. On one occasion, the little building received the Right Rev. Dr. Charles Inglis, the first Lord Bishop of Nova Scotia, who preached from the pulpit during his 1797 visit to Guysborough.

The Anglicans moved quickly to rebuild after the church's destruction. The frame was complete by August 1812, and the new church was soon holding regular services on both Sunday morning and afternoon, although its official consecration did not occur until September 16, 1826. Bishop John Inglis visited in 1827, 1833, and 1834, confirming candidates on each occasion. The 1834 visit remained especially prominent in the memory of the community. On August 10, 1834, he addressed a congregation larger than any previously assembled in Guysborough. Roughly six hundred people filled the pews, crowded the aisles, and gathered outside. Even the Methodist minister gave up his service so that his congregation could attend the auspicious occasion. Between 1877 and 1878, the third Christ Church was erected on the same site. This building is still standing, having served its congregation for almost 125 years. Though it is no longer used for regular services, its wall plaques and windows reflect and preserve the history of the community, and now it hosts a Heritage Service every year, plus special events like weddings and funerals.

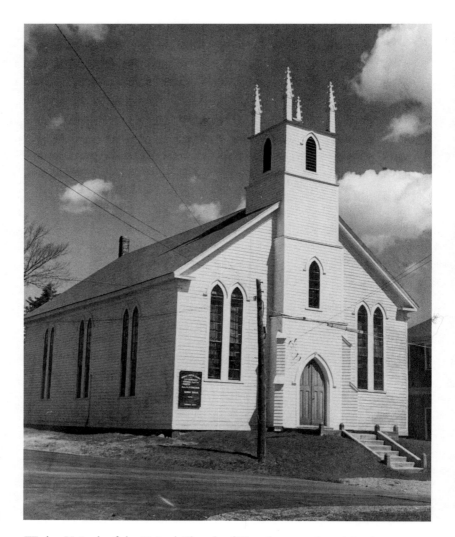

Wesley United, of the United Church of Canada, traces its origins in
Guysborough back to 1808, when the first Methodist clergyman known to
have visited the area conducted a mission here for six weeks. Other itinerant
Methodist missionaries followed, traveling up and down the bay shore from
Guysborough to Canso, administering to the scattered flock. In time, the
Methodists in Guysborough determined that they needed a church building
of their own. In 1828, a public meeting made the decision to move ahead on
a site donated by Thomas Cutler, a local Anglican. The opening services were
held on November 1, 1829. A Mission House or manse was built next door to
house the clergy. The needs of the growing congregation outgrew the building
within thirty years. A new building was erected opposite the old church, on
the corner of Church and Queen Streets, where it still stands. The donation
of the lot by Duncan McColl, a Presbyterian, is an example of Guysborough's
interdenominational cooperation, which has traditionally balanced factional
disputes. Plans were furnished by the junior minister, who had been an
architect, and construction proceeded quickly. The church was dedicated on

August 28, 1858, and has stood in service to its congregation and community for over 145 years. It is the oldest serving church building in Guysborough. The new manse was ready for occupants in 1872. In 1876, the Methodist Sunday School Hall was constructed on the site of the old church (the old building had been relocated to its current home on the shore). The first Mission House was similarly moved from its site to the corner of Broad and Main Streets where it became part of Grant's Hotel. In 1925, a union of the Congregational, Methodist, and many Presbyterian Churches in Canada was negotiated. The Guysborough Methodist Church became part of the United Church of Canada, giving that community and congregation nearly two hundred years in Guysborough to date.

THE UNITED BAPTIST CHURCH ON PLEASANT STREET, 1955

The Guysborough Baptist Church, youngest of the four old congregations in Guysborough, was built by S. J. Atwater and dedicated to the service of God on Sunday, October 26, 1902. The congregation itself is much older, though, dating back to July 5, 1829. By 1832, they had a building under construction, and according to Ray Coldwell, offered praise that "notwithstanding much persecution the good cause is gaining ground, and many souls have been converted." Perhaps due to human frailty, some of the converts soon drifted away and, as early as 1833, "the sword of discipline has severed others from their communion." Nonetheless, the congregation grew in size and resources, purchasing a parsonage in 1866. It supported the Maritime Conference, various national and overseas missions, and Acadia College in Wolfville, NS. There was a revival in 1880, and by 1899 a fund was established to erect a new church building. The construction cost $3,700, and the last payment was settled in 1904 with the proceeds of a Thanksgiving Social, which netted $137. The Baptist Sunday School was organized in 1848, and by 1905 it had registered fifty members, offering a library of over a hundred volumes. Other organizations directly associated with the Baptist Church included the Women's Missionary Association, the Ladies Guild, the Baptist Young Peoples Union, and the earlier White Ribbon Army, whose members pledged total abstinence of alcohol, tobacco, and the use of profane language.

Chapter 2

Travel and Communication

AS REGULAR AS THE TIDE: THE CANN PACKET BOATS, 1928

Hugh Cann and Son Ltd. provided regular packet service from the railhead at Mulgrave to the Guysborough County ports. The service was important both economically and socially important, and included a similar link to Halifax via a second packet system.

Travel and trade were originally conducted by water, but the dangers of the sea increased demands for roads and bridges. Expectations increased as times changed and new technologies were introduced. Guysborough residents demanded railroads and later hoped for airlinks. The use of automobiles changed the countryside, as livery stables gave way to garages, and supply centres changed. Communication was facilitated by improved post offices and telegraph and telephone services. While Guysborough remained at the centre of the personal world of many of its people, that world quickly became much larger and better known than ever before.

THE STAGE-
COACH LEAVING
GUYSBOROUGH
FOR
HEATHERTON,
C.1890S

The need for overland communication routes to Halifax and other communities was immediately acknowledged by the pioneer settlers of Guysborough. In 1786, the High Sheriff, James Lodge, on behalf of the inhabitants, petitioned the Legislative Assembly for funds to build roads. In 1787 the local government decided that the shore of the river would be a public road, and in the following year set aside funds to build a road to what is now Antigonish. Improvements to the local roads came slowly. A later itinerant preacher, on his return from Canso, responded to an inquiry about the welfare of the people there by assuring the questioner that they were fine because "the road was so bad that the Devil himself could not get to Canso."

Gradually, however, roads were laid out, built, and abandoned as centres of population grew and shifted. These roads connected Guysborough to nearby communities and to the outside world. In the days before refrigeration, meat had to be shipped alive to market, and the roads allowed drovers to move cattle, sheep, geese, and other animals to Halifax or other provincial destinations. The concerns about—and the demand for—increased government funding for roads, bridges, and education became political and one of the foundations of the reform movement in Nova Scotia. This movement led to Joseph Howe's rise to political prominence, and to responsible government for Nova Scotia in 1848. In 1858, H. C. Hart reports, the Great Eastern Road from Halifax via Musquodoboit and St. Mary's was extended through Manchester to the Strait of Canso, providing quicker passage to the Strait and a more direct route to the capital. However, even the Great Eastern left a lot to be desired. In February 1848 W. F. DesBarres set out to Halifax to attend the session at the Legislative Assembly. He left Guysborough on Monday and arrived in Halifax the following Sunday—the 125 mile trip took DesBarres and his friends six days. Roads were partly maintained through a 1761 statute labour law that required residents to either personally perform road work for a set number of days per year or to pay for a substitute. Statute labour on the roads was abolished in 1917, but Laurier Grant remembered the Road Section Foreman, Ern Scott, "calling at our door and warning me out to help shovel out the road after a snowstorm."

Winter roads were often abandoned in favour of the ice on the harbour and river. The Municipal Council would annually appoint a "Busher of Ice" whose duty was to mark safe passage between Guysborough and Boylston, and across the harbour to Manchester. The bushing was usually done in December, or whenever the ice was about six inches thick. Spruce trees about six feet long were inserted in holes cut in the ice at one-or two-hundred-foot intervals to provide a guide to safe ice. When horses broke the the ice, as sometimes happened, and the horse and driver could not extricate themselves, the horse or horses "would have to be detached from the sleigh and the animal partly choked with a slip knot about its neck until it became bloated and would then float and be pulled out on firm ice by a few strong men." It was not until the mid-twentieth century that roads were kept open for winter use—though without antifreeze or modern oil, most cars were stored for the winter. Even the contractors who carried the mail reverted to the horse and sleigh, or in the worst conditions, travelled by foot to ensure that the mail got through.

By the time Joseph Howe arrived in Guysborough on horseback in August 1831, the roads closest to town were respectable, but otherwise he described them at best as "indifferent" to "rough and wearisome" where, "unless your beast be singularly sure-footed, both eye and hand are necessary to the security of your neck." While a stage coach service was established in parts of Nova Scotia by 1816, it was likely not until the 1860s that regular coach service reached Guysborough.

By 1862 there were advertisements for a regular stage coach service from Halifax to Guysborough and beyond, "via the new Guysboro road." And in 1885, *Belcher's Farmer's Almanac* informed its readers that "the Coach for Guysborough leaves Heatherton daily on arrival of the mail from New Glasgow and connects with coaches running daily between Guysborough and Cape Canso." At the same time, the Sherbrooke to Antigonish coaches were still making connections at Melrose, with Daniel Seller's Coaches bound to and from Guysborough. The Heatherton–Guysborough stage route continued to be advertised until 1921. Within a few years, horse-drawn stage coaches were no longer used for public transportation. In 1920, the Municipal Council asked the federal government to make the railway station at Monastery a regular stop for passengers and freight, as the councillors considered it the most important and closest shipping point for the municipality. When this occurred, Monastery replaced Heatherton and the "Monastery Road" became the most important highway link to and from Guysborough.

By 1930, Route 16 between the railhead at Monastery and Canso was gravel surfaced, and in the late 1930s it was paved as far as Guysborough. In the late 1940s, the paved road was extended to Canso, and the hard surface was a luxury for travellers. Prior to World War Two, larger trucks began to be used in the area. Highway speed was then, as now, regulated. The Motor Vehicle Act of 1928 demanded that motorists observe a rate that was "at all times reasonable and proper," and added "the Department of Highways considers that a speed greater than thirty-five miles an hour is never reasonable."

A RAILWAY SUR-VEY CREW AT WORK, C.1898

Guysborough never did have a railway. Railroad fever, however, swept the community on several occasions. This survey, taken about 1898, brought some short term employment, but no trains—ever. In the late 1920s and early 1930s contracts were signed, bridge abutments built, and the road bed cleared, levelled, and graded to Guysborough. But the Great Depression struck, the government changed, and the Guysborough Railway was stopped in its tracks. Other than the important few kilometres that linked Port Mulgrave to the Intercolonial Railway system, the entire county was railway free. This was not by choice, as local merchants, residents, and politicians made a variety of unsuccessful efforts to secure rail service.

The Guysborough Railway became a local political joke, the title of a well-read gossip column in a local newspaper, and eventually the subject of story and song: the late great Stan Rogers wrote "There's no train to Guysborough" as a refrain in one of his works. The road bed is today part of the Trans Canada Trail.

A RAILWAY SURVEY TEAM AT WORK NEAR GUYSBOROUGH, c.1898

A survey team for the Guysborough Railway, with the tools of their trade and a great variety of men's headwear. Their instruments include what looks to be a Keuffel and Esser (K&E) transit and tripod, with fixed legs and a rod which would be used with a level for horizontal control. The Y-shaped circle contains a survey chain of one hundred and one feet graduated in tenths, and also marked to measure from the centre of one track to the centre of the second. Several of the crew hold flag or range poles, which are used with the transit to sight in points and, at the far right on its fixed tripod legs, a Gurley or K&E level. Others seem to have shovels or other hand tools necessary to check the grades and mark a possible road bed for a railway. Tools were not the only necessity of the survey, as crews had to be fed and quartered. Even failed efforts brought employment and sales to the community.

In *Along the Shore Road*, Leo and Colin Purcell note that a wooden draw-bridge was built in 1864 to span the Lower Narrows and therefore more conveniently connect the two sides of Guysborough Harbour. The bridge had a "mechanism to lift the centre section to permit vessel traffic" to the upper waters of the Milford Haven River. In 1880 the new municipal government (est. 1879) accepted a tender for the construction of a new bridge which, like its predecessor, was built of wood. In 1902, the Dominion Bridge Company built the steel bridge pictured above. It was usually referred to locally as the "drawbridge" and "it pivoted from the centre to allow for river traffic, and was moved manually with a large crank." When Monastery replaced Heatherton as the closest station to Guysborough, the Monastery road became increasingly important and the "Boylston Bridge" an essential link to the railhead. As vehicular traffic increased, river traffic declined, and the bridge was opened for the last time in 1928, as shipping commerce virtually ended at Boylston. The current is strong in the Lower Narrows and the bridge and its abutments served as a fine stand for fishermen. The drawbridge was replaced by a two-lane bridge, with neither superstructure nor draw.

THE
GUYSBOROUGH
LIGHTHOUSE,
ON THE SHORE
OF CHEDABUCTO
BAY NEAR
THE HARBOUR
ENTRANCE, 1906

Like any seagoing community, there was concern in Guysborough about the safety of the harbour approaches, especially at night or in fog. In February 1842 Robert M. Cutler and seventy-two others (ship owners, merchants and various residents of Guysborough) petitioned the provincial government, explaining that the entrance to the harbour was "rather intricate [and] difficult of access and owing to the want of buoys and a proper landmark or guide, vessels approaching it at night in particular are much endangered." The petitioners requested the creation of a "Beacon Light" at the mouth of the harbour, recommended spots where buoys might be anchored, and suggested that their needs could be accommodated by the expenditure of sixty pounds of public funds. The Legislative Assembly sent the petition on to the Committee on Navigation, and with surprising promptness a lighthouse on the mainland at the harbour's mouth was built by 1843. The building was a small wooden structure, "painted white, with a fixed white light, 30 feet above high water, and visible for eight miles." Before the lighthouse was built, "Mrs. Godfrey Peart had kept a light burning in her dormer window for a number of years, and on many a wild night it was a welcome guide to belated mariners." The lighthouse at Guysborough burned down on September 11, 1904, but it was replaced with another white square wooden building by the federal Transportation Department. The new structure was taller, and its light was visible for eleven miles. It was also equipped with a foghorn to answer "signals from sea in thick weather." Pictured above on July 19, 1906, the Guysborough Light guided mariners for over fifty years. The man in the picture is likely Moses Scott, who Hilda Cox remembers as a "pleasant, jovial man, with a long grizzled beard" who "tended our lighthouse faithfully for many years" and who, upon his retirement, was succeeded by his son, George Scott. By 1930, the lighthouse was augmented by a bell buoy with a flashing light and, on the "stony patch" on the north side of the harbour entrance, a white pole with another flashing light. The last lighthouse keeper was James Jarvis, but he and his family were displaced when the station became automated. Later the lighthouse building was replaced by a simple steel tower. Today the shore again lacks a light, and "belated mariners" can only hope that someone will follow Mrs. Peart's example and leave a light in the window to see them safely home.

Coastal steamers like the *Strathcona* and the *Malcolm Cann* (pictured above) were part of the lifeblood of isolated seaside communities. Carrying freight and passengers to the railhead at Mulgrave, they performed an essential service to the people of Guysborough and the entire shore. Their arrival in port always drew attention, but when the harbour was ice-locked freight and passengers had to be moved, often all the way to Fort Point at the harbour entrance, to get to the ships. The vessels owned by Hugh Cann & Son of Yarmouth, Nova Scotia, served this coast for many years.

GROUP OF MEN INSIDE CABIN OF SS *MALCOLM CANN*, C.1910

Passengers were accommodated on the coastal freighters. While some might be taking the relatively short trip from Queensport to Guysborough, for others it was the first leg of a longer trip by train to "Upper Canada" or the "Boston States," as the *Cann* took them to the railway station at Mulgrave. Grant writes: "Furnishings in the saloon of the *Malcolm Cann* were upholstered in red plush with several bunks for use by indisposed passengers during stormy weather, as well as two private staterooms." These passengers look singularly bored with the experience, so it must have been an easy passage. The man in the apron was probably an employee taking a brief rest.

SS *Malcolm Cann* breaking twoay Guysborough, NS

The SS *Malcolm Cann* was fondly remembered by a whole generation of Guysborough residents. This Cann boat was 112 feet long. According to Fred Buckley, its speed capacity of fourteen knots exceeded the normal nine to ten knots, and the ship was powerful enough to break early ice in the harbour. In Laurier Grant's memory, the crew consisted of Captain Durkee, mate Bob Lipsett, and three deckhands. Chief Engineer Daniel Reid and his oiler and stoker worked in the engine room and stokehold. Grant confirms that this was the fastest of the Cann boats, but he says that it had a cruising speed of ten or eleven knots.

In April 1955, the last trip of the *M. V. Vaneheim*, under the longtime command of Captain Fulgence Bourgeoise, marked the end of at least 170 years of regular service to Guysborough by coastal packets. The first packet on the Guysborough–Arichat run was the *Kingbird*, a sloop owned by Robert M. Cutler. H. C. Hart recounts that the *Kingbird* had been seized near Canso by the authorities for smuggling but, because it was built in the United States, could not be registered and consequently could not continue to be used as a packet. The *James William* soon replaced it and continued the packet service. This vessel was thought to be haunted, as mysterious noises plagued those on board, always stopping when a clergyman stepped on the deck. There is no record of the effect Joseph Howe had on the noisy spirits on his 1831 trip from Guysborough to Arichat on the packet, although some might observe that he had some familiarity with spirits and could be noisy himself.

By 1830, a petition to the Legislative Assembly requested financial support from government for the packet service between Guysborough and Arichat. Suggesting a subsidy of fifty pounds, the petition maintained that the "packet between Guysborough and Arichat (a distance of upwards of thirty miles) to touch occasionally at Canso and Fox Island would afford great accommodation to travellers and all persons in any wise engaged in Agriculture and the Fisheries in this quarter" and promised free passage to the judges of the Supreme Court "when on their circuit to Cape Breton… in a way calculated to afford them comfort and satisfaction." Supported by other petitions from the leading citizens of both Guysborough and Arichat, and financially supported by the local governments of each community, aid was delivered in 1830, and a joint stock company was created to operate the packet service. The service continued to require a subsidy, however, as later requests for assistance claimed that its "Establishment has yielded no profit to your Petitioners." The service was nonetheless maintained, and an Act of Legislative Assembly in 1842 obliged it to carry the mail weekly between the two ports. After the 1880s, with the completion of the railway connection to Mulgrave, the packet service along the coast became a part of the national communication system and was supported by the federal government. Hart points out that when the railway to Mulgrave was opened "the steamer *Rimouski* was put on the route from that terminus to Canso and Guysboro with H.M. Mail." In 1896, "in addition to the *Rimouski*'s trips on Wednesday and Saturday the steamer *Westport* ran from Mulgrave to Guysboro on Monday, Tuesday, and Thursday afternoons, returning on the following mornings." In the 1890s, the contract for the service was awarded to Hugh Cann & Son of Yarmouth, NS. By then, the sailing packets of earlier days were replaced by steam power, and a succession of Cann vessels maintained the service well into the twentieth century.

The other regular packet service ran between Guysborough and Halifax. First supported by the General Sessions in 1841, the business was taken over by Joseph W. Hadley of Guysborough. Between 1846 and 1886 his ships maintained a regular service to the capital carrying an average of one hundred to two hundred persons a year, as well as general cargo and supplies. It was not always a safe trip. In 1848, the *Sylph* under Captain James Gosbee neared the entrance to Halifax Harbour and was wrecked on Devil's Island. The schooner *Guysborough*, launched in 1856, was lost on its second voyage as a packet to Halifax when it struck the Black Prince Rock off Liscomb. The *Lord Eldon* was similarly lost on its maiden voyage, but the *British Pearl*, a seventy-seven ton schooner registered in Guysborough in 1863, made the trip safely for nine years. As reflected in the 1928 advertisement of R. A. Corbett & Co. (p.41), the SS *Chedabucto* was then providing regular weekly passenger service between Halifax and Guysborough with a variety of stops along the way. The steel hulled *Chedabucto* was remembered as a good ice-breaker. Fred Buckley recalled that Captain Cooper would break the ice in Guysborough Harbour: "We always enjoyed going down to the wharf and watching him come up the Harbour, smashing the ice which was sometimes 15 inches thick."

Like the early service to Arichat and then to the railhead at Mulgrave, the packets to Halifax were an integral part of the economic and social life of the community. Before year-round roads were maintained, they were an essential lifeline to the outside world. Harbour traffic was busy, and the regular packets, local fishermen, and merchants were joined by tramp freighters who came and went as cargo demanded. The community also demanded a regular, convenient connection between the two sides of Guysborough Harbour. The roads were bad, and the winter ice, which could provide quick passage, was undependable. During the navigating seasons, local residents wanted a public ferry service instead, and in a petition to the Assembly argued that it "would be of great convenience and advantage to the inhabitants of this County generally." While not as long-lasting as the coastal packets, a ferry boat was often maintained between Guysborough and Manchester from its terminus at Ferry Boat Lane.

GLADYS M. WHIDDEN AND PINK IN GUYSBOROUGH HARBOUR, c.1910

This picture is described by Laurier Grant in *Recollections*. He points out that the larger ship is the *Gladys M. Whidden* anchored and frozen in the ice of Guysborough Harbour, and that the smaller dark schooner is shipbuilder John Sangster's *Pink*. The masts of ships tied up at both Hadley's Wharf and Jost's Wharf (like the SS *Malcolm Cann* at Hart's Wharf) are an indication, Grant suggests, that "the photograph was probably taken on a Sunday." The *Gladys M. Whidden* of Antigonish, "a large two-masted vessel painted white, with a high poop deck" (or stern), was used in the cattle trade. In the days before refrigeration, cattle were shipped live to various destinations, including Newfoundland. "Cattle vessels were generally larger than the usual coasters, as they provided more space below deck where animals could be cared for on voyages when they would be at sea for long periods caused by lack of wind or head winds." Local Guysborough men like Joseph Skinner were employed to feed and care for the animals in transit. Grant explains that hardwood was used in smoke houses of some of the fish plants, and that pit props, used to secure the roof of coal mines, were shipped to the Dominion Steel and Coal Company at Sydney. Products were also shipped into Guysborough. Grant remembers that ships from Prince Edward Island would arrive in October and November with oats and vegetables, and that people within a twenty-mile radius would bring carts to buy a winter's supply. Coal was also landed from the coastal sailing vessels, for both domestic and commercial use.

ADVERTISEMENT, 1928

Coastal freighters were essential to the life of the community. From the 1820s to the 1950s, Guysborough was a regular port of call of these vessels. The Cann Company ships made regular connections to Mulgrave, the mainland terminus of the Intercolonial (later the Canadian National) Railway. The ships of R. A. Corbett and Company Limited, as noted in their 1928 advertisement, maintained a regular link to Halifax.

Building Millers Cove Bridge. Guysboro, Nov 1912. MaB Photo.

BUILDING THE MILLER'S COVE BRIDGE ON SHORE ROAD, 1912

The earlier Miller's Cove bridge was swept away in the August Gale of 1873. This new bridge, built in 1912, was later replaced by one of concrete but today is largely abandoned. The road on that side of Miller's Cove, named for Christian Miller, an early settler and prominent innkeeper and office holder, is no longer in public use.

A SEAPLANE ON GUYSBOROUGH HARBOUR, c.1929

Not even the ravages of the Great Depression destroyed the optimism of the municipal leaders of Guysborough. The roads were still not open in the winter, the railway was virtually a dead issue, and the packet boats, carrying mail, passengers, and supplies, provided the only regular communication with the world. Nonetheless, in 1939 the Municipal Council petitioned the Federal Government for the construction of an airport within the Municipality, as those at New Glasgow and Sydney were too distant to be convenient. Although not successful, perhaps the petitioners had been inspired by this seaplane landing on the harbour in 1929. In May 1927, Guysborough residents watched Charles Lindburg fly over in the *Spirit of Saint Louis* on his epic journey across the Atlantic. The aircraft here has been identified as a British-built DeHavilland Model 60 Gypsy Moth.

EVELYN FRANCHEVILLE WITH THE FAMILY BUICK, C.1958

The first automobile came to Guysborough in about 1905 and, as it was the first opportunity many people had to see one, there was excitement over what many considered a passing fad. Public attitudes were not universally positive, as evidenced by a 1913 municipal bylaw that prohibited motor vehicles from being on public streets on Mondays, Wednesdays, Thursdays, Saturdays and Sundays, leaving owners only Tuesdays and Fridays to drive their cars. The penalties for not obeying the law were fifty dollars for a first offence, one hundred dollars for a second, and two hundred dollars or sixty days' imprisonment for a third offence. At a time when "a dollar a day was very good pay," such penalties were oppressive.

Despite the law, automobiles were owned in Guysborough. Laurier Grant remembered that one of the first was owned by W. H. Cunningham of Cunningham Brothers' Store in Guysborough, and a second by "A. J. (Sandy) Bruce of Boylston who had been in the lucrative business of operating a rum shop in Guysborough." In 1916, Grant and his brother, in business together, purchased a brand new Model T Ford from A. J. (Phonse) Gillis of Eastern Auto of Antigonish. Gillis arrived in Guysborough with the car on a Saturday afternoon, obviously in defiance of the bylaw. He explained how the car worked to the proud new owners, accepted their cheque for five hundred dollars, and the deal was done. Neither permit nor licence was required. The car had to be started by crank and was fuel-fed by gravity. It sported magneto lights, lacked both a speedometer and windshield wiper, and demanded a good supply of spare tires and lots of blow-out patches.

The McLaughlin Buick, pictured here, was purchased new in 1929 by Christopher Francheville of Guysborough. This Silver Anniversary model was built in Canada, and cost between three and four times as much as the Ford Model A, the most popular car in 1929. Christopher Francheville's son William (Billy) was a mechanic and took his father's new car apart as soon as he had the chance; to the family's relief he reassembled it again, correcting what he considered to be faults in its original construction. He must have done a good job, as the car continued to be driven by the family until 1966, and is now almost four decades later is undergoing restoration so that it can be enjoyed once again. Here Evelyn, Christopher's granddaughter, is displaying her trophy from a family fishing trip.

STREET SCENE, WITH HORSE TEAM AND WAGON ON MAIN STREET

Cars were popular but expensive, so most people continued to rely on the tried, tested, and true, using horses for both work and travel. The horse and wagon were still familiar sights on the streets of Guysborough well into the 1960s.

Main St.
Guysborough Nova Scotia.

MAIN STREET FROM ABOVE, C.1933

A busy day in town. Rollie Johnson's new garage and its gasoline pumps were obviously part of the centre of attention, and automobiles of various makes are evident. The flat lot to the left of the garage was the site of the pre-fire Masonic Lodge. This picture is dated about 1933, and was likely taken from the roof of the post office. The number of cars and people suggests that an important event was afoot. Indeed, August 22, 1933, was election day and Clarence (Clary) Wentworth Anderson (1871–1944) of Sherbrooke, who ran under the Liberal banner, won the contest and represented Guysborough County in Halifax until his resignation in 1937.

Grant's Hotel
Guysboro, N.S.

GRANT'S HOTEL ON THE CORNER OF MAIN STREET AND BROAD STREETS, 1932

In his famous *Rambles*, Joseph Howe spoke well of the accommodations Guysborough provided. Travelling on horseback on the uncomfortably wet day of August 3, 1831, he wrote, "Before we are quite drowned, we enter the village of Guysborough, shrouded in mist and smothered in showers; and, by the advice of a fellow wanderer, betake us to the most respectable public, over which Squire Christian Miller presides." Miller was one of the pioneer settlers and an old soldier, the High Sheriff of Sydney County, and kept the best inn in the area. It was not the only public house, as several were licensed at one time or another. Being a publican was apparently not without danger. In 1787, both Miller and Hugh Hugh were licensed to keep public houses in town by the Court of Sessions. On the same day, Hugh Hugh entered a plea of guilty to a charge of assault and battery "committed on the body of Christian Miller" and was fined five shillings.

Joseph Howe considered himself fortunate in his billet as, when he found his luggage had not withstood the rain, Mrs. Miller rescued him. He recounts: "Stretching ourselves in a large armchair in front of a blazing fire, we fell fast asleep, and was just dreaming of half-drowned mariners, snatched from the billows by kind damsels to share the warmth and comfort of their cots, when we were roused to behold our gallant host, charging by the side of the mighty Frederick [the Great of Prussia] at the battle of Prague," and to be regaled with stories of the Seven Years' War. Public houses, or inns, were sometimes ranked by the quality of sweetener provided to their clients. First-class establishments served white loaf-sugar, second-class served brown sugar, while the lowest on the scale served no sugar at all and only molasses was grudgingly provided. In a time before rapid transportation, inns and public houses were more frequent, but because there were also fewer travellers, many were part-time ventures. For many years, Grant's Hotel was both the best and the best known (and sometimes the only) hostelry in the community. It was established in 1870 by John and Anne (Dennis) Grant, in what had been her parents home facing Main Street on the corner of Main and Broad, the latter being locally know as Dog Lane and was part of what was once called Irish Town. Beyond the Hotel there was said to be a rum shop and two taverns and it was well known to the local constables as a place where many fights broke out. It was here that Lame Bill Skinner sometimes removed his wooden leg to use it with devastating effect on his opponents.

In 1872, when the new Methodist manse on Church Street was finished, the Grants purchased the old house and had it moved to their premises, where it became an addition to their hotel. Likewise, the building that had been Anne's father's shop was altered to become the dining room which overlooked the harbour. Upon the death of this generation, the hotel became the property of their niece, Nellie Grant, who married Sheriff Wiley Smith.

In 1941, Charlie and Hilda Jenkins purchased Grant's Hotel and ran it until 1986. Faced with increased competition, heavy expenses, and a faltering business, the hotel was closed after nearly 125 years in business. In the fall of 2003 the building was torn down.

MISS ROBBY OF
THE WESTERN
UNION
TELEGRAPH
COMPANY IN
GUYSBOROUGH,
1899

Miss Robby in the Western Union Telegraph office in 1899. Note the board which controlled the twelve lines of the office, the telegraph key, and on the right the counter to receive messages for transmitting. A boy would be employed to deliver telegrams to locals.

The North American development of the telegraph is credited to American painter and inventor Samuel F. B. Morse. The first Canadian telegraph company was formed in 1846, and in 1851 the Nova Scotia Electric Telegraph Company was incorporated by some of the province's leading entrepreneurs. They immediately contracted the construction of a line from Pictou to Sydney for £5,500. By November 13, 1851, the section to the Strait of Canso was completed and, while the crossing was a challenge, the wire was soon stretched all the way to Sydney. In 1854, a line from Antigonish to Canso via Guysborough was constructed and H. C. Hart maintains that telegraph service in Guysborough was available in 1855. The Guysborough office was officially opened on January 1, 1856, in the lower part of William Moir's house. Its first operator was Margaret McGregor from the village. The Nova Scotia company was first leased and then sold in 1872 to the Western Union Telegraph Company, and at some point the Guysborough office was closed. Service was restored, however, on February 19, 1876, when the Dominion Telegraph Company opened an office with Charles Barss in charge of the land line. This and any later development of telegraph szystems in Guysborough was due to the creation of trans-Atlantic cable systems. A. A. MacKenzie points out that while the first trans-Atlantic cable landed in Newfoundland, and from there to northern Cape Breton, others came to the Guysborough coast. In 1875, a cable connected Ireland with New Hampshire (and Guysborough), and in the 1880s both the Western Union and the Commercial Cable companies landed cables that connected Great Britain, Europe, and the United States through their offices in Canso and Hazel Hill. In 1879, the Western Union Telegraph Company advertised that it controlled "all of the telegraph lines in the United States and the Maritime Provinces, from Port Hood to San Francisco, and connecting via Atlantic Cable and Northern line with all the telegraphs in the world." By 1900, many of the nineteen trans-Atlantic cables in operation were routed through Guysborough County from Canso and Hazel Hill, where operations were maintained on a twenty-four hour per day schedule. Such an extensive operation provided employment for many in Guysborough, as goods, services, and employees were needed. However, the cables were shut down by 1962, superceded by more modern technology. Over those years, however, the cables made the area one of the world's great centres of communication and much of the public and private news of the world was known here first.

"NUMBER
PLEASE!" MRS.
EVELYN BRYSON
ON SWITCH-
BOARD DUTY,
1956

Mrs. Evelyn Bryson worked the switchboard that connected the telephone system. In this January 1956 photograph Mrs. Bryson, with headphones and microphone in place, is poised to fill a customer's request. Many young women (and a few young men) sat at the switchboard to connect callers with their intended audience. The operator also directed calls to members of the Fire Department if an alarm was called in, provided news on an infinite number of topics, could track down the doctor, police or other emergency officials, and generally provided assurance that there was life within the telephone service.

Commercial telephone services began in Canada in 1877, and the Nova Scotia Telephone Company was created in 1888 and became part of the Maritime Telegraph and Telephone Company in 1910. Many communities had purely local systems (by 1900 there was a four telephone system linking Goldenville, Sherbrooke, Sonora, and Wine Harbour, and before 1908 there was a two telephone system in Canso) before they were connected to the Nova Scotia Telephone Company's lines. By 1905, the Antigonish and Sherbrooke Telephone Co. was extending its system. By 1908, the lines of the Antigonish and Sherbrooke Telephone Company Limited had reached Guysborough, and in that year they were also extended to Canso. Its 1909 *Subscriber's Directory and Schedule of Rates* points to central offices maintained at Antigonish (at the Nova Scotia Telephone Company's office), Goshen, Guysborough, Goldboro, Sherbrooke, Marie Joseph, Canso, and St. Andrew's. In 1909, 13 of the 288 subscribers listed were in the village of Guysborough. Dr. George E. Buckley had a telephone in both his residence and his office but most of the other telephones were in businesses. The first "Central Office" in Guysborough was located in the home of John E. (Johnie) Lawlor, who also operated a livery stable. The office remained in this location for many years until it was moved to the residence of Colin Bryson, where it remained until 1974 when an auto-mated system meant the Central was closed. In the early years of the system the Central Office operator was simply asked to connect the caller and the called by name. This became impractical as the service grew and telephone numbers were introduced. New ideas are not always gracefully accepted. In response to one caller's request to be connected to "Markies," the operator reminded her that Mark O'Connor's store was number one, which prompted the caller's rebuttal: "He may be number one with you, dear, but he's just plain old Markie to me." In 1909, normal telephone service extended from 7:30 A.M. to 10:00 P.M. six days of the week, and from 9:30 to 10:30 A.M. and 1:00 to 3:00 P.M. on Sunday, although the lines were "always open for urgent calls." Subscribers were pointedly reminded of the ethics of telephone use, and particularly that the use of the "party line unnecessarily on Sunday disturbs other people."

The telephone quickly became an essential part of modern life. In rural communities "mutual" telephone companies (in which subscribers—some-times as few as seven—owned their own system) and "Central Offices" like Guysborough became the point of connection with the Maritime Telegraph and Telephone Company through which coast-to-coast linkage became pos-sible in 1920. By 1956, telephone cables stretched across the Atlantic Ocean, and today thousands of calls are handled in a system that links communities like Guysborough to the entire world.

GLUED TO THE MIRACLE: TELEVISION IN WALTER BUCKLEY'S DEN, c.1950s

Radio was the first modern communication miracle of the twentieth century, opening a whole new world of news and entertainment to isolated communities and breaking the monopolies of the newspapers as the only means of informing the public. In Guysborough, Walter Buckley built his first radio, which was likely also the first in the area, in 1922. The "crystal" radios of the 1920s needed earphones to hear the reception and were soon replaced by more powerful battery or electric powered models. While eventually superceded by television during the so-called golden age of broadcasting (1925–1950), radio was a major source of family entertainment for a while. Events like royal visits, elections, on-the-spot reports like the 1936 Moose River gold mine accident, and war news were avidly reported and followed as the Canadian Broadcasting Corporation's (CBC) trans-Canada radio system meant more Canadian content.

The television age began at the end of the Second World War, and the CBC began broadcasting in Montreal and Toronto in September 1952. Later that decade, Guysborough got its signals from Sydney, Cape Breton. The first person in town to own a television was Walter Buckley. This was of enormous interest to the children of the community, who beat a path to Mr. Buckley's door. He made all welcome, and as this picture shows, his den was often crowded. A smaller group than on many occasions, the television watchers (from left to right) in the back row here are: Joe Phalen, Ann O'Connor, Ronnie O'Connor, Helen Jones, Margaret Grant, and Craig Buckley; in the front row: Gordon Jones, John Grant, Jamie Grant, Kenneth Halloran, Bernice Jones, and Eric Jones.

Chapter 3

Business and Industry

NON-UNION WORKERS, C. 1915

Despite the claims of some that the people of Guysborough made a living by taking in each other's laundry, business houses were established to engage in the import and export of goods, including the produce of the sea, the forest, and the farm. While small by provincial standards, they were important to the community as many depended on them for a living. Workers were needed to run the shops, farms, mills, and woods camps; sailors and fishermen to work the ships at sea. Many people may have filled all of these roles during their working life and, like the men in this picture, been jacks-of-all-trades. These non-union workmen, with the tools of their employment, are ready and available for hire.

SHIPBUILDING
AND SHIPPING
OUT: THE JOHN
J. SANGSTER
SHIPYARD
c.1880

Here John J. Sangster both built and repaired ships. Sangster's yard was one of several in Guysborough, where wooden sailing vessels of various types and sizes were constructed.

Guysborough was the centre of a shipbuilding industry that extended from the village up and down both sides of the harbour and river. From the 1840s to the 1930s, it was a port of registry. A Lloyd's of London insurance agency representative also had an office here, which added to Guysborough's local significance within the industry. The first ship constructed after the French occupancy of the area was by Loyalist merchant William Nixon in the 1780s. Just over one hundred years later, the "last vessel of size" built in Guysborough was on the stocks in John J. Sangster's shipyard at the foot of Pleasant Street.

Between the 1780s and 1880s, dozens of ships slipped into the waters of the harbour for the local fishing industry, the coastal trade, or the ports of the Seven Seas. Captain Charles Maguire remembered that "in the place where Laurier Grant's [Chris West's] new house now stands, was a ship yard. Some of the vessels built there were schooners *Selph* 1846, *Betsy* 1847, *Guysborough* 1848, *Isabelle* 1849, *British Pearl* 1862, *Little Belle*, *Garnet*, and the last in that yard was the *Josie* 1883." Further along the shore the brig *Acadian* was built while the Jost yard contributed, among others, the *Annie Roy*, *Estelle*, *Laura*, and *General Gordon*. Some of the other shipyards in Guysborough were the Sangster business and that of Francis Cook where, H. C. Hart points out, between 1836 and 1849 the brigs *Manchester*, *Guysborough*, *Eliza*, *Francis*, and *Active*; the schooners *Speculator*, *Harriet*, and *G.O. Bigelow*; and the 350-tonne barque *Medora* and the 520-tonne barque *Atlantic* were all launched. Other records show over 130 vessels equalling 12,650 tons built in Guysborough and vicinity. In 1865, there were 54 vessels registered at Guysborough which, when compared to the 297 at Yarmouth, the province's largest port of registry, is small but of enormous importance to the local economy.

Vessels were built on the basis of 64 shares per ship to allow for a number of owner partners and to reduce economic risk. While some were built for owners elsewhere and some were built to be sold, many were built to be sailed. Local construction, local owners, local captains, and local crews meant that all parts of the industry played an important role in the local economy, and its decline left a hole that proved difficult to fill. The list of lost ships and men was long, and when tragedy occurred within a closely related community it affected everyone. In 1840, the schooner *Agnus*, built and owned in Guysborough, sailed from Halifax to Jamaica and was never heard of again. Captain John Graham left a wife and two children in Guysborough; crewman Henry Morgan, from a large local family, was lost as well. In 1846, the *Murdocks* went down on a voyage from Guysborough to Fortune Bay, Newfoundland, and Captain William McKeough, with crew members Robert Giles, John Grotto, James Ehler, George Hadley, and Charles Roberts—all Guysborough men—were lost. Captain McKeough's son William and son-in-law Captain James Bruce, sailing together, were similarly lost some years later. Likewise, the brig *Plover* under Captain James Gosbee left Halifax bound for the West Indies in March 1854, and was lost. Gosbee's wife and six children waited for him in Guysborough and the wife of one of the crew, Mrs. Cole, also watched for her husband's return. Many more ships and men, however, came and went safely. Despite the risks and hardships of work and life on any craft, young men signed on and sailed from Guysborough into and out of local and international ports. Many worked in other countries, of course, and a large number were among the Nova Scotians that sailed out of Gloucester, Massachusetts.

The vessel on the stocks was built in the John J. Sangster shipyard in
Guysborough; the name of the vessel was kept a secret until the launch took
place. Hilda Cox related that during its construction people would ask John
Sangster "what her name was going to be, and he always put them off by
saying, 'Oh, that is a mystery.'" A launch was always a great event, and Cox
writes that one of her earliest memories was "sitting on the grassy slope with
a great many other people" on August 30, 1890, to see *Mystery* slip out of her
stocks and into the waters of Guysborough Harbour.

In this picture the keel of *Mystery* has been laid, the ribs are in place, and
the planking is underway with a crew of ten workers busy, although some
of them have paused for the photographer. A lot of work is yet to be done
before launch day. Obviously the planking, caulking, decking, etc., must be
completed. Usually the masts were stepped, the rigging installed, the sails
put into place, and the cargo loaded only after the launch but depending on
high water, on occasion this was all completed on land. The launch was an
especially nerve-wracking experience for owners and builders. It seems that
the vessel could be insured while under construction and when afloat, but
not during the transition from land to water. Accordingly, after the skids were
well greased and the naming ceremony concluded, the blocks were driven out
and the held breath of the onlookers was exhaled in a cheer when the vessels
slid cleanly into the arms of the waters, and congratulations were offered all
around.

The *Mystery* has clearly taken shape. It was schooner rigged, having one deck and two masts, carvel built, with a square stern and a billet head. It was about 98 feet long, just over 26 feet wide and had an 11 foot hold. Its registered tonnage on September 18, 1890, was 190.47, but some years later it was re-measured for insurance purposes and due to some internal changes was recorded at 162.50 tonnes. Its recorded owner on the day of the launch was Master Mariner John J. Myers of Manchester, who held all its sixty-four shares; by September 1893, however, Henry Marshall Jost was the sole owner of the *Mystery*.

The ship was built to transport cargo and it went wherever trade took it, rarely returning to Guysborough. Between 1895 and 1896, for example, it visited ports all over the world, including: Boston, Massachusetts; New York; Georgetown, South Carolina; Barbados; Puerto Rico; Antigua; Trinidad; Rio de Janeiro; St. Thomas, US Virgin Islands; Jordan River, Saudi Arabia; Demerara, Guyana, and many ports in the Atlantic Provinces. The ship transported a wide variety of goods, from sugar to sheep manure. Captain Charlie Maguire remembered the *Mystery* as a very fine ship, and wrote that "she loaded cattle in Guysborough three successive Mondays. I personally remember that it was considered a big day for us young boys the day the cattle boat was loading."

TAMING THE FIRE: HULL'S FORGE AND BLACKSMITH SHOP, C.1895

In the days of horse power and sailing ships, the smith was an important artisan. Located on the waterfront, Hull's forge and blacksmith shop, which Cook suggest dates from 1838, was in a good location to make or rebuild the metal components of ship construction or repair. The smith was usually also a farrier and could both make or adapt the shoes and shoe the horse. While some smiths specialized in some part of their trade, most could perform a great variety of tasks. If you needed andirons for your fireplace, special shoes for your driving horse, a new metal rim on your wagon wheel, a pot repaired, chains reworked, or a place to gossip and get the latest news, the blacksmith's shop was the place to go. Many smiths effectively changed with the times: when ships converted to steam or diesel motors and automobiles replaced horses, smiths became the mechanics that continued to keep the world moving. A good blacksmith was a respected member of the community that depended on his skill. This building is no longer standing.

M. H. Davison was the editor of *The Guysborough Gazette*, a weekly newspaper that ran from 1894 to about 1908. The paper, which came out (at least in 1895) on Fridays, carried a subscription cost of one dollar a year. It contained items of provincial news, general news, many advertisements, and as much local news and views as it could obtain. Like most local papers, it had the task of keeping up with all the latest gossip as the main purveyor of local news. Some years earlier, John J. Scott printed and edited the *Guysborough Star*, a weekly that ran from 1880 to 1883. It was Davison who opined that while Guysborough might have been "laid out" as a city, it had not been buried! The four women and their roles in the *Gazette* offices have not been identified, but the fact of their employment in the late 1890s is in itself significant.

THE HARTSHORNE CARDING MILL ON CUTLERS BROOK, MAIN STREET, C.1900

In an age when local produce had to be processed by local industry, a variety of mills dotted the country. Saw mills, grist mills, and the carding mill illustrated above were essential to the livelihood of forest and farm. The job of a carding mill, here run by waterpower, is to clean and comb the fibres of wool, hemp, and flax into order so that the spinning and weaving can take place. Elizabeth Pacey points out that "at one time in the days of waterpower, there were more water wheels churning in Nova Scotia than in any other province or state in North America." In 1851, eighty-one water wheels were powering weaving and carding mills in the province, a number that rose to ninety-nine by 1870. The mill in Guysborough had been operating for over fifty years when it appeared on the 1876 A. F. Church and Company map of the county. The mill was operated by three generations of the Hartshorne family, and was likely in the hands of Lawrence Hartshorne when this picture was taken. While busiest in the spring after the sheep were sheared, many carding mills extended their season by weaving cloth for sale or exchange, and by re-carding and selling the "shoddy" or leftover wool that had accumulated on the machines. As transportation facilities improved and technology advanced, many of the small local carding mills could not compete with comparative giants like the Windsor Cotton Company or Stanfields, and they closed their doors. This mill was sold to the Sonora Timber Company in the 1920s with the other Hartshorne holdings. The carding machinery was acquired by Ben Morrow of Boylston, who operated it in conjunction with his saw mill and grist mill. A second carding mill was operated in Guysborough until about 1950 by the MacKeen family at the site of their saw mill. Most of its product went home to the spinning wheels and looms of busy rural women, to be made into "homespun" cloth for clothes for their families, or into yarn for mittens, socks, underwear, toques, and sweaters. As a reflection of the importance of politics, Charles MacKeen remembers that the Conservatives tended to take their wool to Hartshorne, while the Liberals tended to deal with the MacKeens. There was also a grist mill run by the Morgan family and located on Morgan's Brook that ground local grain for over one hundred years.

This mill, located on what was then called Cutler's or Carding Mill Brook, beside what is now the main road into town, was not working when this picture was taken, as the water flow has been diverted from the wheel and is running onto the ground, under the bridge, and into the harbour.

"THE SHEEP ARE IN THE MEADOW," BELMONT FARM, C.1930S

When photographer W. R. MacAskill visited the Guysborough area, he took a number of photographs that featured sheep. The raising of sheep had been touted as one of the agricultural routes to economic salvation for the county. On December 19, 1885, the special correspondence of the morning *Halifax Herald* contended that "What Guysboro Wants" was a few knowledgeable emigrants, as there were "thousands of acres of grazing" for "hundreds of thousands of sheep." This photograph was taken from Belmont farm, with Guysborough in the background. The "special correspondence" may well have included these sheep among the "superior flocks we witnessed" in "perfect condition." At any rate, their owner would have appreciated the convenience of the local carding mill.

**A NANNY AND
HER CHARGES
ON A FINE DAY
FOR A WALK,
C.1900**

While most black people farmed, fished, worked as sailors, laboured in the woods, etc., employment outside of their own homes for black women generally meant working in the homes of white people as domestics, as cleaners or in this case, as a nanny looking after the children of her employer. Paid employment opportunities were scarce for women generally, and those for black women were even more limited.

THE JOST FAMILY MERCANTILE HOUSE (1823–1990), C.1900

The mercantile house of the Jost family began in 1823, and shopping at Jost's Store became a tradition for generations of local residents. In 1822, John Jost and his cousin, William Moir, both shoemakers, came to Guysborough from Halifax seeking employment. They were kept busy here during the summer, and Jost felt that the prospects of the community were such that he wanted to be part of it. In the spring of 1823, in silent partnership with his brother George, he returned to Guysborough with a supply of goods and established a shop. Another brother, Christopher, accompanied him and, partly disabled from birth with deformed feet, was the bookkeeper for the business. In the fall they found that they had done so well that they procured more goods and returned to Guysborough to stay. Christopher purchased George's interest and J&C Jost was born. By 1827, the brothers had obtained the four water lots which remained the long term site of the business. In 1838, the brothers separated amicably, both remaining in business in the village. John established the "British House" nearby, and Christopher retained the original site and premises. Eventually, two of Christopher's sons purchased the business from their father and it became B&G Jost, the name it held to the end. The business had a lot of customers, many of whom were carried on credit for up to a year. Payment by cash was the exception in the 1880s. As noted in the *Maritime Merchant*, "The business was essentially a bartering business, every article in the store having marked on it three prices, the cost price in code, the cash selling price and the trade price." Accounts were settled by the acceptance of a wide variety of goods including butter, eggs, meat, fish, feathers, tallow, and woollen goods such as mittens, socks, and homespun cloth, as well as shingles and horse collars. Butter was an especially important trade item, a fact attested to by the inventory item of 535 butter tubs purchased from local Mi'kmaw coopers and sold to local farmers. Some customers brought in as much as one hundred and fifty pounds of butter at a time in tubs of forty pounds or more.

THE NEW JOST STORE, ERECTED IN 1929

Even more important were fish for the Halifax market, and beef and pork—often cut up and salted—for the Newfoundland trade. The business did not just sell and receive goods; it also sent its own ships to the fishing banks of Newfoundland and engaged in the coasting trade. In 1890, the Jost brothers replaced their old store with a fine new four story building built by local contractor George Y. Grant at a cost of three thousand dollars. Grant liked the Second Empire architectural style. Many of his buildings—residential, institutional, and commercial—were built in accordance with its features.

His son, Laurier Grant, remembered that the business carried an extensive inventory of goods (except tobacco, as Burton and George Jost, ahead of their time, banned its sale in any form). The business also had flour and feed storage buildings near its wharf. The comfortable homes of both Burton and George Jost were on the hill above Main Street. Hilda Cox commented that "Burton was a great Baptist and a great Liberal, while George was a great Methodist and a great Conservative. It made a very satisfactory arrangement."

CHRISTOPHER A. JOST (1879–1952), C.1930s

In a spectacular and disastrous fire in December 1927, Jost's Store burned to the ground. The local fire department worked mightily to keep the fire from spreading, but were unable to save any part of the building itself. Despite this setback, owner-manager Christopher Jost, in the spirit of his forefathers, erected a new store in 1929. The new premises were smaller and not as showy. B&G Jost remained in business until noon, June 30, 1990, under the later management of Gordon Drysdale and Earl Wright.

The building is still standing, a centrepiece of the waterfront development, but it is no longer connected to the name of Jost. While the one hundred and sixty-seven year life of the Jost mercantile house was the longest in the history of the community, it was not the only such business. The Cunninghams, the Harts, the Condons, the Morrisons, the O'Connors, the Buckleys, and others all maintained long term businesses in the village, helping to make it the commercial centre of the district.

THE BRITISH HOUSE, ON MAIN STREET, c.1900

The British House was the shop established by John Jost after he and his brother Christopsher split their common business. The shop was later owned and operated by his son Henry Marshall Jost, who sold it to Robert Morrison. Four generations of Morrisons used this building before it was acquired by the Mulgrave Road Theatre Company for its use. In this picture, Robert Morrison and his family are comfortably tucked into their horse drawn sleigh. The building next door was later moved and the house, built for Henry Marshall Jost, was the home of the Morrison family.

THE SHOP OF W. H. BUCKLEY AND SON, WATCHMAKERS AND JEWELLERS, C.1910

The store and residence of W. H. Buckley. To the left is the barber shop of Daniel Gould, later run by William "Bill" Shea. To the right was the Gould residence, where Mr. and Mrs. Percy Moulton later ran an ice cream parlour and offered room and board to paying guests. William and son Walter Buckley operated their shop from 1894 to 1968. The clock above the door was the symbol of the watchmaker just as the striped pole marked the barber's shop. Gould, customer, and the man with the horse and cart all paused to ensure their place in the picture. The inside of Buckley's store, to young eyes, far more interesting than the outside. This picture suggests that cruet sets were a popular item on the shelves as were vases, pitchers, cups and saucers and clocks. The curved glass display case on the counter contained pen and pencil sets, watches, rings, and other finery. Walter Buckley also tested eyes

and fitted glasses, as well as carrying on his father's trade of watchmaker and jeweller. They also had some books available; it was here my mother purchased *Big Farmer Big* for me at age five, as compensation for the indignity of the required smallpox inoculation before beginning school.

**THE MACKEENS'
MILL, ON THE
MILL BROOKE,
c.1910**

Three generations of the MacKeen family operated a mill in Guysborough for over eighty years. A tannery had originally been established by the Hart brothers on this site. William and Tyrus Hart were involved in trade, a staple of their business being salt beef, and Newfoundland was one their principal markets. As hides were a by-product of the salt beef industry, a tannery was built to make use of them, with brother Joseph Hart in charge. The availability of leather led to the establishment of a shoe factory under the direction of tradesman John Hunt of Halifax, and the training of numbers of young men from Guysborough as apprentices in this industry. Robert MacKeen and William Whitman, his partner and brother-in-law, ran the tannery and for some time tanned hides for the local shoe and harness makers. They also ran a shingle mill, carding mill, and saw mill. After the dissolution of the partnership, the MacKeens produced sawn lumber for domestic use as well as export, and shooks for fish boxes demanded by the fish plants down the shore. The MacKeens had men working in the woods cutting timber. The timber was then milled at their mill, and exported from their wharf on ships they owned, leased, or hired. Between 1896 and 1967, MacKeen's Mill was a local institution which, along with its distinctive mill whistle, was part of the sights and sounds of the community.

CHILDREN HAULING WOOD, c.1910

The line between work and play was very narrow for yesterday's children. These children are hard at work bringing home firewood with their sleds. The shafts, which on another day might be fitted to a dog, are here handled by boys. The sleds themselves were likely used as much for coasting down Guysborough streets as for working.

THE LEWIS HART STORE ON MAIN STREET, C.1913

Lewis Hart's ancestors were Loyalists, and arrived with the pioneers who established themselves at Guysborough. His father's shop was located across the road near the present-day location of the Wonder Store. The Hart home was originally located on the site of the new store, and the property ran to the harbour where Hart's Wharf and the family's warehouse were located. In 1913, Lewis Hart built this fine new shop between B&G Jost and Robert Morrison's "British House." The retail outlet was just one aspect of the business. Hart was the local agent for the various packets that connected Guysborough with Port Mulgrave and Halifax, and these and many other vessels tied up at Hart's Wharf. He also bought fish, which were cured on flakes extending from the shop to the wharf, from local fishermen. In addition, he sometimes had vessels of his own engaged in trade with Newfoundland and elsewhere. On this day two horses and wagons are stopped in front of the business. The warehouses can be seen below the new building. Earlier residents of Guysborough referred to business outlets as "shops" and to warehouses as "stores," so when early commentators speak of large stores they are making reference to places of storage. The "shop" was later purchased by the Sonora Timber Company and later, when the Company went bankrupt, by Vladimir Drouginine and John MacIntyre. The building was purchased by B&G Jost after the death of Drouginine, a Russian émigré who escaped the Russian Revolution of 1917 and settled in Guysborough.

INTERIOR OF THE LEWIS HART STORE, C.1913

The public space of the store amounted to this one large rectangular room. Encased in the decorative impressed tin which was then popular, and furnished with counters, shelves, and drawers, it contained merchandise in barrels, boxes, bags, and jugs.

CLEANING UP AFTER THE STORM: AN OCTOBER GALE, c.1917

Although the August Gale of 1873 was the worst natural disaster to befall the fishing and coastal fleets, severely damaging the wharves, stores, and other structures of eastern Nova Scotia, other gales caused considerable damage as well. Captain Charles Maguire remembered the October Gale of 1900 as being very severe. He told how the coal shed on Hart's Wharf, which contained about seventy-five tons of coal, was blown across the roadway. He also described how the schooner *Fama*, tied up at Morrison's Wharf, broke adrift and sank. This photograph reflects the power of the elements on one schooner, shown with its rigging entwined with the other, having taken on water and keeled over. Luckily the shallow water kept it from sinking. The two workmen are no doubt measuring the task facing them in the restoration of order, which included pumping out the hull and disentangling the lines of the swamped vessel. The building of wooden sailing ships had a resurgence in the years after 1910 through the 1920s because the demand for steel brought on by World War One meant they were cheaper to construct and run. The days of wooden ships and iron men would soon pass again, however, as the longer life of steel hulls and the dependability of steam and diesel motors displaced the older technology.

THE *E. M.*
***ROBERTS*, 1920**

The number of board feet and general tonnage of wood that was produced in Nova Scotia, plus the percentage that was exported to foreign markets, must have perpetuated the myth of the limitless forests of the New World. Wood in the form of deal (which would be later re-sawn), shingles, lathes, spars, and other goods were usually wanted and often protected in Great Britain and, even after the end of the timber preference, Nova Scotia products were competitive in the British marketplace. This trade extended into the twentieth century. Captain Charlie Maguire, remembering the local timber trade, commented, "When the square rigged ships would come in and anchor in Hall's Cove, take off their sails and spend a month or more loading the ton timber; the load in the hold would be taken in thru bow ports."

The export of wood products by ship extended well into the twentieth century. In 1920 the three-masted schooner *E. M. Roberts*, which could carry about four hundred thousand board feet, loaded a cargo of long lumber from G. Y. Grant and Sons for St. John's, Newfoundland at Jost's Wharf. In addition, the two-masted schooner *Lena* was tied up at Morrison's Wharf, taking on box shooks from the Grant mill for the National Fish Company at Port Hawkesbury. Other ships were occupied carrying lumber, shooks, pit props, and firewood from the port for construction, fish boxes, coal mines, and the smoke houses of fish packers along the coast. By the 1920s, however, the export of pulp wood became the single most lucrative product from our forests and from the port of Guysborough, and it was tied to the advent of the Sonora Timber Company.

The year 1917 was a dark one. Canada was suffering a political crisis tied to the desperate need for more manpower to fight the war that many believed was the "war to end all wars." The fighting itself was horrendous, with bloody battlefields and trenches that stretched for miles. Even worse, in Russia the Bolsheviks had staged a successful revolution and overthrown the government of the Czar and withdrawn from the war. While the Allied forces regrouped and won the war in 1918, the after-effects of the Russian Revolution were felt in far away Guysborough. Among those forced to flee the Revolution were five former naval officers who met in New York and gained control of a number of Russian steamships that were tied up there. They subsequently formed the Polarus Shipping Company. The officers were led by T. N. Agapayeff and, seeking cargo for their ships, learned there was wood available in eastern Nova Scotia and a market for wood pulp in the United States. By 1923, the Sonora Timber Company had set up pulp operations in Sherbrooke and Sonora, and shortly thereafter established offices in Baddeck and Guysborough.

Fred Buckley remembered that one of the "most exciting times" was when they started shipping pulpwood from Guysborough. The pulp boats, up to 325 feet long, were almost "twice the length of any boat we had ever seen before, and it was quite exciting to see these ships coming up the harbour." The size of these ships meant that the harbour entrance had to be dredged in order to get twenty feet of water so these ships could take a full load of pulpwood out at high tide.

After purchasing or leasing wood land, the Sonora Timber Company built a rossing mill Lower Salmon River and purchased Lewis Hart's General Store in Guysborough for their own use. They invested more than three million dollars in the Company's business and were likely the largest pulp operation in the Maritimes at the time. The names Agapayeff, Drouginine, Vorapayeff, Riazanoff and Truchininov became familiar names in Guysborough County, especially to the 1,000 to 1,500 workers in eastern Nova Scotia who were on the payroll at different times. The Sonora Timber Company was an important factor in the total economy of the area as one of the few employers in a time of economic depression. The Company, however, folded about 1932 due to the worsening economic conditions and to technological change, although some wood was still being exported in 1936 by their receivers. Long after any direct economic impact of the Company existed, its influence was still felt in Guysborough as the Drouginine and Vorapayeff families became long-term residents. Forestry retains an important place in the economy of the Guysborough area. Today, however, logs, pulpwood, and Christmas trees are carried by trucks to be processed elsewhere, and the timber ships and pulp boats no longer come into Guysborough harbour to take on cargo.

The *New Brunswick No. 1*, the dredge brought in about 1922 to deepen the harbour channel, tied up at Jost's Wharf. The stores and shed of Jost's and nearby Sonora Timber Company Wharf (previously Hart's Wharf) are also evident, as is the overturned boat in the backyard of the residence next door. The use of large ships by the Sonora Timber Company made it necessary to deepen parts of the harbour to allow easier access to the wharves to load and unload these vessels.

SONORA TIMBER CO., LOWER SALMON RIVER, c.1924

One of the rossing mills of the Sonora Timber Company. This mill was located at Lower Salmon River; company ships carried the product to markets in the United States. The company was a major employer in the Guysborough area in the 1920s and early 1930s. A rossing mill removed the bark from pulp wood prior to its shipment.

Selling newspapers was one of the ways that young boys made pocket money or, in other cases, directly contributed to the family economy. A succession of young people hawked or distributed newspapers, including the *Saturday Evening Post* (shown here in about 1928), likely in the hands of Lloyd Buckley. Jack Smith, at another time, also sold the *Post*, while Arthur and Laurier Grant sold the *Montreal Standard* and the *Chicago Ledger* "for which there was good demand. The latter had a lot of sensational news of murders, robberies, etc…as well as a serial which many read each week." Other popular weeklies included the *Family Herald* and the *Star Weekly*. Still others, at different times, sold magazines like *Liberty* and *Chatelaine*. Other newspapers that were popular were Halifax dailies the *Chronicle* and the *Herald*, which were read depending on one's political affiliation, various denominational papers, including the *Presbyterian Witness*, as well as the *Eastern Chronicle* from New Glasgow, the *Casket* from Antigonish, and of course local papers like the *Gazette* and the *Canso Breeze*.

LOADING CHRISTMAS TREES, GUYSBOROUGH, c.1930

Today scores of trucks pass through Guysborough carrying Christmas trees to markets in New England, central Canada, the West Indies, and elsewhere. For many years, Christmas trees, like all other trade goods, were taken by ship. The production and loading of this product for a once-a-year market provided wages to a number of workers, both men and boys, in the cash-strapped days of the Great Depression—although stevedores may only have received ten cents an hour for a ten hour day. The number of buildings on the waterfront attests to their importance to the community's business life. This picture is probably of the Hofford Christmas Tree Company.

THE CUNNINGHAM BROTHERS' STORE, 1932

After renting space on the first floor of the Masonic Hall for some years, the brothers John and William H. Cunningham built their new premises in 1900. Their wharf and "store" were located harbourside behind this building, the large front windows of which provided an opportunity to advertise their wares. The small windowed door to the left of the pumps was for some years one of the telegraph offices, while the attached Cunningham House could accommodate travellers. The Cunningham warehouse was built on their wharf. On one occasion, carefully noting where some kegs of seized alcohol were stored, some locals took their dory under the warehouse, drilled through the floor and into the kegs, draining them into their boat before silently rowing away to enjoy their unusual catch. The building is no longer standing.

D&M WHARF, GUYSBOROUGH, ON A WINTER'S DAY, C.1935

The D&M Wharf, together "with its water front, warehouses and general store on Lower Main Street," had been the Lewis Hart property. It was purchased by the Sonora Timber Company and then, after the Company folded in the early 1930s, the property was acquired by Vladimir Drouginine and John MacIntyre, respectively the former purchasing agent and the former paymaster of the Sonora Timber Company. They ran their new business under the name D&M. The wharf continued to be the berth of both packet boats and freighters until the packet boats ceased operation and the cost of the wharf's maintenance outstripped its revenue. In 1957, the federal authorities built the new "government wharf" which replaced the Jost Wharf and the D&M Wharf with a single pier. On this winter day, two ships have tied up, the ice having been opened either for or by them.

The older Hart property had served a few different functions. Steam-driven coastal vessels required a sure supply of fuel, and coal was landed at Hart's Wharf and stored in a large building known locally as the "coal shed," owned by general merchants L. E. Hart & Co. They also acted as agents for the Cann steamboat line. Coal was also sold to householders in Guysborough. "It was sold by measurement and not by weight and hoisted from the hold in large tubs which were emptied into two wheeled dump carts, each taking a load of one half chaldron." The five to ten chaldrons (at thirty-six bushels per chaldron) needed to heat a house over the winter were carted by local entrepreneurs like George Tarbot, Cranswick Desmond, Nate Skinner, and Lame Bill Skinner. Laurier Grant also recalled that "while coal was being delivered it was a source of income to many of the boys about town who were employed to shovel it in the coal bins."

**THE BON TON
TEA ROOM ON
MAIN STREET,
C.1938**

The Bon Ton was an institution for several generations of young people in Guysborough. For thirty-five years, the tea room of Cornelius (Connie) and Gladys Payne was the place to go for a snack, play the jukebox, see others, be seen, and just to hang around. While the inner tea room was generally reserved for older customers, the front room—with its booth and joint confectionary and serving counter—was generally crowded with young people. Many a romance was developed here, and the flick of the lights that signalled the end of the business day was accepted with resignation at best. The building had an apartment on the second floor above the business and this picture also shows the ice house on the rear left. On the right is the building that served for some years as the Legion Hall.

Chapter 4

Sport, Recreation and Societies

SKATING ON CUTLER'S COVE, C.1920S.

The pioneer families in Guysborough had little time for idleness. First land had to be cleared and stumps uprooted, crops sown, houses built, the fishing grounds investigated, and the prospects of trade explored, for these were the basics for survival; then citizens focused on establishing schools and churches. Recreation was only allowed after work was completed, and even then the first "fun" activies—hunting, fishing, and gathering—were based on old necessities. Then these pioneers, many of whom had come from very established communities, had time to celebrate their cultural heritage, including leisure interests and pursuits.

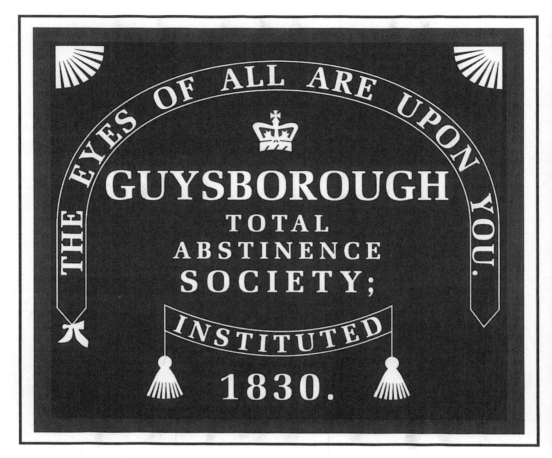

THE EYES OF ALL ARE UPON YOU.

GUYSBOROUGH
TOTAL
ABSTINENCE
SOCIETY;
INSTITUTED
1830.

BANNER OF THE TOTAL ABSTINENCE SOCIETY

The Temperance Movement was no doubt the strongest social movement in Nova Scotia since the religious revivals of the previous century. The concern about the negative impact of rum did not arise out of prudishness, but rather in reaction to the private and social price of its over-consumption. In those days, many considered rum a necessity of life in the damp, hostile climate of Nova Scotia, and prodigious quantities were consumed. One commentator observed that the "household keg in the cellar with its spigot and mug were as common a sight as the potato bin or the barrel of salt herring." In Guysborough, the response was the establishment of the Guysborough and Manchester Total Abstinence Society in 1830. This society flourished for a number of years and, according to H. C. Hart, it was "the means of reclaiming some and restraining many from intemperance." In 1831, Joseph Howe commented that he was informed by a "good authority, that the Temperance Society would never have taken root in the place, had not the delicious currant wine, which the ladies make, reconciled their husbands to the abandonment of more ardent but less palatable beverage."

Society meetings were held in the courthouse in town, and in many of the rural communities as well. These were often popular social events. Addresses on temperance were solicited from visiting dignitaries and local clergy, and outdoor festivals were held during the summer, with parades of the local groups proudly displaying their banners and flags. Women, who often suffered because of their husbands' heavy drinking, were foremost among the supporters of the movement. In Guysborough, they formed an integral part of the Society, and purchased material to make three banners. The ladies' banner was of white silk bordered in blue and bore the gold-coloured satin lettering: "Temperance, we love the cause," and "It is good to be zealously affected always in a good thing." The men's banner was of blue silk edged in red, with the motto "The eyes of all are upon you" in a semicircle around a crown with the organization's name below. The boys' banner, in plain white, bore the inscription: "United we stand, divided we fall," and on the reverse: "Boys, be true to your pledge."

This movement was not supported by everyone. On the night of April 15, 1839, shots were fired into homes in both Cook's Cove and Guysborough by unknown and undiscovered assailants. The provincial government offered a hundred-pound reward which was never claimed, but it was determined that the attacks were perpetrated by persons in favour of the liquor trade, intended to discourage temperance magistrates from prosecuting, and in retaliation for fines imposed for illegal traffic.

The temperance movement had interdenominational support, even if the membership was not always representative. Following the directive of his Bishop and the example provided in Antigonish, Father Richard J. Meighen, parish priest at Guysborough, established the St. Ann's Temperance Society sometime between 1841 and 1845. This society flourished under his direction, and it too held annual processions in the summertime as a way to promote its message. After the parade, lunch was served on the glebe house lawn and music was provided by local fiddlers.

On February 13, 1851, the Chedabucto Division, No. 93 of the Sons of Temperance was organized in Guysborough. This was a relatively new organization in the province, and it grew quickly until it had divisions in most of the eighteen counties. The three organizations co-existed, and together fought an uphill battle against liquor. In 1856, armed with a petition signed by 150 women, the ladies of the movement called upon the Grand Jury not to grant any more licenses to sell spirituous liquors.

In 1857, a Band of Hope was organized for the young people, and in 1859 the Chedabucto Division of the Sons of Temperance purchased the Kent Church to use it as their headquarters for many years. While the Grand Division of the Sons of Temperance met in Guysborough in 1868, it did not mean that the battle was won. In 1876, the Deputy Grand Worthy Patriarch of the Manchester Division of the Sons of Temperance reported that "here we have no open enemy in our midst to contend with" and that they were willing to help battle the enemy in Guysborough, but the people there would not "lay hold of the work." In the shire town, the Manchester DGWP reported that there were about six rum shops and "not *one* fine had been inflicted" that season. The 1878 passing of the federal government's Canada Temperance Act allowed municipal governments to decide on the legality of the retail sale of liquor. By the 1890s the nationwide popularity of the temperance lodges was in decline, but the battle went on in Guysborough. In 1895, Mrs. Burton Jost was the local president of the Women's Christian Temperance Union (WCTU), the most important temperance society for women, and one of the few organizations through which women could play a political role. Despite being on the ebb of its popular tide, the greatest successes of the temperance movement came with World War One, when prohibition became identified with patriotism and the war effort. In 1915 and 1916, most provinces prohibited the retail sale of alcohol until the 1920s, when it was resumed under government control. In 1933, the end of prohibition in the United States virtually killed the hopes of the diehards left in the movement.

In 1903, the Guysborough Sons of Temperance disbanded and latersold Chedabucto Hall. The local option remained, however, and except for the Legion Hall and the government-owned liquor store, no liquor licences were issued for retail sale until the growing tourist industry demanded it.

THE GUYSBOROUGH BICYCLE CLUB, c.1895

There is no record of when the first bicycle appeared in Guysborough. A bicycle club was formed in the 1890s, however, so it is likely that the two-wheeler, in one of its various forms, had been present for some time.

The Guysborough riders were part of the "Great Bicycle Boom," a fascination that reached its heights in the 1890s, and which brought a degree of independence, especially to young women, that no doubt shocked the matrons of the Victorian age. Bicycles had arrived in Nova Scotia by the late 1860s, and the styles available moved from the aptly (if ominously) named Paris Boneshaker to the penny-farthing high wheelers to mass-produced safeties with pneumatic tires. The number of young men and women with bicycles in this picture says something about local prosperity as a new Falcon No. 3 bicycle ordered from the 1895 Eaton's catalogue cost eighty-five dollars, while the ladies model, the twenty-one pound Falcon No. 4, chain-driven like the men's but with a lower rail to accommodate long skirts and front and back guards to prevent those skirts from being caught up in the chain, cost ninety-five dollars. When the wages paid to adults are considered, it is clear that both would be beyond the expectations of most young people, yet the number of riders and "wheels" shown above suggest the importance of both the bicycle and the fad to the young people of Guysborough.

A NICE DAY'S CATCH: SPORT FISHING IN GUYSBOROUGH, C.1900

Local or visiting sport fishermen had the option of harbour, bay, river, or lake to pursue their pleasure. Here the successful fisher displays his catch for the camera. By the time of this photograph, while a catch of trout made a nice meal, most people no longer depended upon each day's catch for sustenance. The introduction of European brown trout into Guysborough Harbour by Dr. John Bonsall Porter increased the popularity of the area for sports fishermen, bringing employment to local guides and visitors to the community.

Women in Nova Scotia enjoyed opportunities to meet together in societies and organizations. While some of these were auxiliaries to fraternal or service groups like the temperance societies, women also created or joined female-based organizations. Their purpose often lay within the traditional sphere of what was considered a woman's role, and were concerned with charitable and other good works. In Guysborough, this role was represented by the 1823 establishment of the Guysborough Branch Ladies' Bible Association by Charlotte Newton. A long-time Guysborough resident and local school teacher, she was the moving force in a number of interdenominational organizations and movements. She was later remembered as zealous, undeterred by opposition, and "indefatigable in her efforts to promote every good object." Charlotte Newton was supported by other women of stature in the community like Mrs. Thomas Cutler, the Association's first secretary-treasurer, and they worked to ensure that every family had a copy of the scriptures.

Acutely aware that preparation for eternal life and the immediate needs of current life were not always compatible, the women of the Bible Association moved to manage these pursuits as well. At a meeting in 1824, the distress of a local family who had lost both their home and four of their children in a house fire was discussed. The meeting decided to devote an afternoon to making clothing for the survivors, and that each woman would bring materials for the work. When this was accomplished, it was proposed that the work sessions be continued on the first Monday of each month so that there would be a reserve to supply anyone in need. This was the origin of the Ladies' Benevolent Society, which provided assistance to friends and neighbours for many years. The two societies moved on together. The work was so important to Mrs. Cutler that, upon her death in 1832, a "handsome donation" was left to the "work basket" and her daughter became her successor in the position

Depositary. The two societies split in 1839 when the members belonging to the Church of England withdrew, and the monies and material belonging to the Benevolent Society were equally divided. The Society continued, with Charlotte Newton as Secretary. Her minutes described meetings that lasted from 2 P.M. to 9 P.M. with intermissions for tea, formal business, and a devotional closing which was often led by a member of the local clergy. Otherwise, all were busy sewing and the extent of their labours is revealed by the items distributed in the first fifty years of the Society's life. Between 1824 and 1874, the Ladies' Benevolent Society donated over 2400 garments, 35 large quilts and 8 cradle quilts, 4 bed ticks, 10 sheets, and yards of material, shoes, boards, nails, feathers, and groceries. The Bible Society had also been made a separate organization in 1833 (again with Ms. Newton as Secretary) and it too continued its work. In its first fifty years it raised 425 pounds in support of its mission and with new generations of leadership, it continued its work well into the next century.

In groups like these, including the organizations supporting local churches like the Ladies Aid, the Women's Missionary Society, and the United Church Women, women moved outside their busy lives to contribute to their community together. Their role in other organizations like the Home and School, the Red Cross, and the Temperance Society was such that in Guysborough, like elsewhere, women were the backbone of the community.

THE GNC HOCKEY TEAM, C.1908

Hockey has been described as Canada's greatest contribution to winter sport and a major preoccupation of Canadians for over a hundred years. While contradicting claims over its birthplace rage on, there is no doubt that the game itself has been played in almost every part of the country. Before covered rinks, artificial ice, and electric lights, hockey was played on whatever stretch of ice was available. In Guysborough, this often meant games on the frozen coves of the harbour and consequently without boards, although pictures of matches on Cutler's Cove show a triangular rink clearly set off on the ice. Star skates, made in Dartmouth, NS and considered to be the best in the world, were available at Marshall Jost's store and contests were arranged against other communities, including Mulgrave. Hockey was also played on Mussel Cove, an outdoor rink on DesBarres Pond with boards and electric lights, and on the edge of what we called the Cowboy Woods. Hockey was a school sport as well and in the winter of 1933 the eight players of the Guysborough Academy team defeated Canso 2–0. In the 1960s the Guysborough Combines continued the tradition of hockey in Guysborough.

SUMMERTIME AT HOME, C.1910

A gazebo or summer house on the grounds of Dr. George Buckley's home on the corner of Main and Pleasant Streets, overlooking Guysborough Harbour. Enjoying a break from his busy practice, Dr. Buckley is joined by his family and friends. This often included his daughter, Abigail, and son-in-law John A. Tory. Like his brothers, Henry Marshall and James Cranswick Tory, John left Nova Scotia to make his livelihood, and like them he maintained a close relationship with his home area. Eventually, John Tory purchased the lot next door, where the John J. Sangster Shipyard had been, and built a summer home.

GUYSBOROUGH WOMEN'S BASKETBALL TEAM, C.1913

Basketball was invented by Canadian James A. Naismith in 1891 as an indoor winter recreation sport for his students at the YMCA International Training School (now Springfield College), in Springfield, Massachusetts. It has become an international favourite with a huge fan following. Of the nine students in Naismith's first class, five were Canadian and three were from Nova Scotia, and they brought the new game home with them. By the turn of that century, basketball was played in YMCAs, schools, universities, and the armed forces, and Nova Scotians have eagerly participated in the sport ever since. Women's basketball soon followed, and "Girl's Rules" were developed in 1894, which were intended to reduce the roughness of the game. These rules were used in Nova Scotia until 1966 when "Boy's Rules" were adopted. Women were playing organized basketball in Nova Scotia at least as early as 1910 and likely earlier. Nonetheless, this picture of a women's basketball team in Guysborough in January 1913 would still rank it as one of the early representatives of the sport.

For a community built on a snug North Atlantic harbour, where many inhabitants made their living on the sea, nothing could be more natural than a consuming interest in boats. Because pleasure often follows work, trips to and from the fishing nets often became a contest of speed, endurance, and ability. The distinctions of best rower, best sailor, and later the most powerful motor, were points of honour to be hotly contested. Even after the number of commercial fisherman operating out of Guysborough declined, the interest in boats continued and many families maintained yachts for pleasure and racing.

On June 6, 1895, the *Guysborough Gazette* reported that the Queen's birthday had been "generally observed as a holiday here," and that a prominent feature of the day "was the first annual regatta of the Royal Club on the harbour." The competing boats were W. H. Buckley's *Lulu*, G. A. Peart's *Iona*, C. M. Francheville's *I.X.L.*, and R. P. Cunningham's *Bretwalda*. The three-mile race included "two kite shaped routes from the stake boat to windward around the big island first and the little island second," and was won by W. H. Buckley in thirty-five minutes. The Regatta became an annual event in the sporting life of the community for the next forty years. August 16, 1913, was a Regatta Day in Guysborough, and people gathered from the entire area to join in festivities. Many of the observers gathered on Regatta Hill next to St. Ann's Church for games, entertainment, and conversation, while out on the harbour the boats and their sailors prepared for the races that would capture the attention of most of the patrons. In its heyday, the Regatta attracted large crowds of spectators and competitors from up and down the shore, as well as from Guysborough itself.

Yacht "Dreamer" Guysborough N.S.

THE PRIDE OF THE BUCKLEY FAMILY: THE YACHT *DREAMER*, C.1920S

The *Dreamer*, with sails unfurled and ready for a peaceful sail or a race. The *Dreamer* was built by Fred Buckley, brother of William H. Buckley. Fred Buckley was a violin maker who worked in Boston and later in St. Louis. He built three sailboats before he was twenty, the last one being the *Dreamer*. The yacht was twenty-eight feet long. It had been built twenty-four feet long, but on one of Fred Buckley's visits home, likely about 1900, he cut it in two, added four feet, and built a cabin on it. The yacht was canvassed and double-planked in about 1912. It was "a flat style boat but very fast," and a popular participant in the casual races and formal annual Regatta held on Guysborough Harbour. After some years of storage in the Buckley boat house, it was sold to a buyer in New Glasgow. It is said that the old timers were sad to see it leave Guysborough and watched it go with tears in their eyes.

Many families maintained yachts or some other kind of water craft. The sail boats were joined by motorboats before 1916, when Laurier Grant purchased the sixteen foot *Mona* from Bill Atwater of Boylston, who had bought it from Charlie Maguire of Guysborough. Grant used the boat for both pleasure and profit, and said that the *Mona* was the first motor boat to be owned in Guysborough. Fuel for the *Mona* had to be brought from Halifax by coastal freighter in forty gallon steel drums.

The winner of the races organized by the Guysborough Nautical Club was honoured by receiving the John A. Tory Trophy. This handsome trophy, today part of the collection of the Old Court House Museum, is a suitable reminder of the days of the Guysborough Regatta and the yacht racing tradition.

It is now impossible to determine when horses were first raced on the ice of Guysborough Harbour. However, it is likely that informal races had occurred by the 1850s. By the 1890s, the quality of local horses was such that a group of Commercial Cable employees at Hazelhill purchased a champion Standardbred in Antigonish County to compete against "the unbeatable Guysborough horses."

In the early 1950s, winter racing was a deeply ingrained institution and attracted contestants both locally and from other communities like Antigonish, Mulgrave, Queensport, Port Hood, Judique, and elsewhere. By the 1950s the races were mostly held on Broad Cove at Boylston on Wednesday afternoons when the village stores were closed.

Jack Shea was the dean of the racing set. His "Brendan's Boy" was a familiar name, as were "Willardale" and "Texas Girl" owned by Leo and Arthur Kennedy, brothers whose four sons were all racing enthusiasts. Jim Larabee, the bank manager—whose son Paul later set a world age/class record—was a consummate horseman, and his little bay gelding "Wayne Budlong" was a consistent winner. A race could hardly be held without Ed Haley of Antigonish, and from Mulgrave came competition from the Camerons, Peoples, Ryans and Jellows. Norman Borden was a regular competitor, as were Harry Jones ("Danny Boy"), Bill Shea ("Buster Clegg"), Harry George ("Heiny") and Went Peart ("Buzzaway"). Queensport fans could cheer for "Peter at Court" owned by Czerney and Garnet Reynolds, while those from Larry's River and Lundy often supported their own local entrants. A good turnout from Canso could be counted on, and the opening of the Canso Causeway allowed Cape Breton fans to attend. A number of others competed, including Del George, Garfield Gosbee, and George Grant, who first raced his own horse ("Roy's Pal") at age eleven. Pat MacKinnon, who drove several of Ed Haley's horses, and Ellen Campbell, driving her own big chestnut gelding, were two young women who also competed. No one loved the sport more than Russell Williams, who raced "Royal Admiral" and "Buster Clegg" in the 1950s. Sadly, the ice is empty now.

Adapted with permission from *Frozen toes and the Sport of Kings* by Jamie Grant.

COASTING, c.1920s

Most coasting was done in the winter, when sleds and toboggans of all kinds were brought out of summer storage and treated to a good wax polish for increased speed. The first fall of snow meant building snowmen and snow forts, making snowballs, and coasting on the hills of the village. Coasting seems to have been especially troubling to the lawmakers of Guysborough. In January 1849, a regulation against it was passed and ordered to be posted in two of the most public places in town. The new law stated that:

> Every boy or other person found coasting or sliding on the snow or ice on sleds or sleighs or otherwise howsoever down the hills or any of them in particular on the following streets in the Town of Guysborough namely Broad Street, Church Street, Presbyterian Meeting House Street, Moirs Lane, Chappell Street, Cunninghams or Post Office Street, Water Street, Main Street, Franchevilles Ally, shall be subject and liable to a fine not exceeding five shillings for each offence to be chargeable on the parent or parents of any child underage—and the Master or Masters of any apprentice respectively...

However, it would seem that even such draconian efforts did little to curb the participation in this winter pastime. In Hilda Cox's memories of her life in Guysborough, she fondly describes coasting down the streets of Guysborough. She writes that:

> Before the days of paved streets and snow plows in winter...what wonderful hills these were for coasting. The snow would be packed to a smooth slipperiness, and the hills would be covered with children and sleds of all sizes and ages. Jost's Hill [Presbyterian Meeting House Street] was the most exciting as it was steeper, and often one could go across Main Street and way out on to Hart's Wharf, that is, if one could steer well, or otherwise

[one could] meet with disaster. Even the grownups would enjoy coasting on McColl's Hill [Main Street] on moonlit nights. The older boys would procure a horse sled (used for hauling cord wood), and one boy, lying face down on a small sled, would take a whole big sledload of coasters down the hill. There were no motor cars in those days. The only danger was from horses and sleighs. But sleigh bells could easily be heard, and there was always someone on foot who could call out a warning.

A WINTER'S DAY ON THE TOBOGGAN, c.1920s

When increased numbers of automobiles made it too dangerous to use the roads for coasting, many hours were spent on the hills with single sleds, bob-sleds, and toboggans, and any child who found a new sled, or even a "coasting auto" wagon, under the Christmas tree was fortunate indeed.

**BERRY-PICKING,
c.1920s**

Picking blueberries provided a good day's outing for families. The berries would be eaten raw, used in baked goods, or preserved for the winter. For many, however, berry picking augmented the family income as berries of all kinds were sold door-to-door in Guysborough to pay for school supplies and other items. It was common to find an elder daughter of the household sent off with the younger children to the berry field to give their mother an opportunity to get some work done. Laurier Grant commented that one of the uses of locally made barrels was the storage of berries: "Red berries provided valuable vitamin C for their usually large families during the long winter. A barrel or more of red berries, which resembled cranberries although smaller, could be kept for many months by merely covering them with cold water." Berries contributed to the wellbeing of the entire family.

Scott Farm
Guysboro. N.S.

THE SCOTT FARM ACROSS THE ROAD FROM BELMONT, c.1925

The "rural" was a short step from the "downtown" in a village like Guysborough. The Scott farm, later the home of provincial agricultural representative Ross Bury and family, is an example of the close proximity of town and country.

Agriculture has been an essential part of the life of Guysborough from its first days. In 1831, nearly fifty years after the establishment of Guysborough, newspaperman Joseph Howe commented that he expected Guysborough to be a "tolerable Fishing Settlement," and admitted that he never heard the community mentioned "unless in connection with pickled fish and oil." However, the settlement had an agricultural base as well. In fact, the reason immigrants received land grants was to encourage a society based on an orderly agricultural model rather than the unsettled timber trade or the uncertain fishery. But government plans went awry. In 1821, John Morrow, the secretary of the Guysborough Agriculture Society, complained that due to the immediate advantage of the lucrative fishery, farming "was lightly esteemed and totally neglected."

This situation was not peculiar to the Guysborough area—John Young, the agricultural writer who published under the name "Agricola," pointed to the backward state of agriculture in the province in letters which were published in the *Acadian Recorder* beginning in 1818. In response, the provincial government created the Central Board of Agriculture, with John Young as its secretary. The government also created the Guysborough and Manchester Farmer's Society, organized on June 4, 1819. Local societies and the Central Board, prompted by government, worked to convince farmers of the importance of their work and the need and means of its improvement. Guysborough had a close association with the Central Board, as Young, although living and working in Halifax, became the MLA for Sydney County (which then encompassed what today are Antigonish and Guysborough counties) in 1824 and held the office until his death in 1837.

While these factors no doubt had an impact on the agricultural prospects of the area, they did not bring immediate change. Thomas Chandler Haliburton (1829) praised the "superior quality" of the land on both sides of the harbour, but lamented that it had "never been subdued by the plough" nor fertilized. Haliburton went on to note that the inhabitants, aided by the "spontaneous fertility of the soil," raised "black cattle, horses and sheep, in considerable numbers" and exported several cargoes of them to Newfoundland every year. Otherwise, the surplus agricultural production of the area was limited to "great quantities of butter" and some oats and potatoes. Like Morrow, Haliburton attributed the state of agriculture to the bounty of the fishery in Chedabucto Bay, which he described as "perhaps as productive as any in the known world."

Agriculture became part of the trinity of farming, fishing, and forestry, which formed the economic basis in the Maritimes. The existence of organizations like the Guysborough and Manchester Agricultural Society gave

CREW OF THE
TREADMILL-
DRIVEN
THRESHING
AND WINNOW-
ING MACHINE
INVENTED BY
ZENAS LANE OF
KENTVILLE IN
1837, C.1900

agriculture a special prominence. The "Reserve Lands" at Manchester were placed under its superintendence, prizes were awarded for farm produce, ploughing matches were organized, and cattle shows were held. Inspectors from the Central Board of Agriculture visited local farms and submitted reports. Prizes were awarded for improvement and innovation. In later years, the society purchased bulk fertilizer for its members, and used a small government subsidy for the maintenance of a breeding bull for the area.

The society did not always enjoy unanimous local support. In 1853, Edward I. Cunningham and 162 others signed a petition asking the Legislative Assembly to reassign the annual twenty-five pound grant to the Agricultural Society (which had "proved of little or no practical benefit") to the maintaining of a public ferry across Guysborough Harbour, which the petitioners agreed would be a "great convenience and advantage." This struggle suggests that agriculture had not advanced beyond the marginalized role it had held a decade before.

It also could have represented the interest of the new Lieutenant-Governor. Lord Dalhousie had been keenly interested in agriculture and was a patron of Joseph Young (Agricola), and according to Joseph Howe his example "set all the councillors, and officials, and fashionable mad about farming...They went to Ploughing Matches—got up Fairs—made composts and bought cattle and pigs." However, governors changed, and "when Sir James Kempt came he had a passion for road making and pretty women, and the agricultural mania died away. Agricola was voted a bore...and the Heifers about Government House attracted more attention than the Durham Cows." Without the patronage of the Lieutenant Governor, the agricultural societies stumbled. They did not recover until another Lieutenant Governor revived the interest in the 1850s when, Howe contends, everyone became interested in "Alderney Cows and Shanghai Chickens," which was not surprising for "Prince Albert was a great breeder, and the Queen [Victoria] and everybody else went mad about poultry for a summer or two."

MASONIC HALL, MAIN STREET, 1928

Freemasons generally agree that the 1717 establishment of the Grand Lodge of England was the beginning of their organized society. The Masonic Order spread quickly from England to other countries, and British colonials brought the organization to North America. While some American Revolutionaries like Benjamin Franklin and George Washington were Masons, so too were some Loyalists and disbanded military men who established Guysborough. Despite the trials and duties of creating a new settlement, the Masonic Lodge, "Temple No. 7," was organized in January 1785. A. C. Jost points out that Captain William Grant was the first Master of Temple Lodge. He had been a member of the Regimental Lodge of the 22nd Regiment of Foot, with the ranks of Past Master, Royal Arch Excellent Mason, and Master Mason. Others, like "Worshipful Bro. Campbell" (later Sir William Campbell), were no doubt also involved in the organization prior to the creation of Temple Lodge.

The meetings were first held in local inns, then later in the large second floor room in the new residence of one of the members. In time Temple Lodge lost its charter, but the Order was re-established in 1875. Hart says that young men who had been members of Lodges elsewhere moved to have one again in Guysborough. On March 30, 1875, the "Eastern Light Lodge" opened under a dispensation, and was chartered on June 7, 1876. They first met in the same room that brethren of the earlier Temple Lodge had used many years before. Eastern Light Lodge No. 72 was a subordinate lodge of the Grand Lodge of the Most Ancient and Honourable Fraternity of Free and Accepted Masons of Nova Scotia. In 1879, W. S. Peart was the Worshipful Master and C. C. Hart was Secretary. In 1882, the Lodge built its Hall on Main Street. The large building had three suites of offices on the second floor which were rented to various professionals, likewise the large space on the first floor which was commonly used by a merchant. The Board of Trade rooms and a telegraph office were also housed within the building as were, of course, the Masonic rooms themselves. This building was destroyed by fire on July 13, 1933, and the Lodge purchased the Chedabucto Hall of the Temperance Division, which had disbanded in 1903. The Eastern Light Lodge and its sister organization, the Eastern Star, have been a part of the life of the community for one hundred and thirty years, while the history of the Masonic Order in Guysborough extends over a period of two hundred and twenty years.

THE DESTRUC-TION OF THE MASONIC LODGE BY FIRE, 1933

Towns of wood regularly faced the tragedy of uncontrollable fire. Here, on July 13, 1933, the local brigade was out-duelled by fire when the imposing Masonic Hall, a landmark on the main street, was consumed. Many of the contents have been rescued, but the single hose of the local volunteer fire department was faced by too much fire and the handsome building was destroyed. At this fire, as is the general case, there seems to be as many spectators as workers.

Backyard
W.H. Buckley Res.
Guysborough Nova Scotia.

GUYSBOROUGH GARDENS, 1932

As early as 1831, Joseph Howe commented that in Guysborough "gardening is a favorite amusement" and complimented the "tasty arrangement and agreeable disposition" of the plots of vegetables, noting that "flowers are fostered" as well. A hundred years later in 1932, "the tasty arrangement" of the flowerbeds and trees in W. H. Buckley's backyard ran between his house on Lower Main and the harbour's edge. The rustic splendour of other gardens, such as B. L. Parker's, attested to the tradition of gardening.

THE SALMON HOLE, C.1950

For many people of succeeding generations, summer meant treks to the Salmon Hole to swim. The salt water warmed in late summer and early fall, and Miller's Cove, Tory's (earlier Sangster's) Wharf, etc., were used. But the Salmon Hole, with its high rocks and nearby grassy areas where swimmers went to dry off or to picnic was a favourite. Both boys and girls learned to swim at these sites, and went to Salmon River Beach or Clam Harbour Beach to enjoy the bonus of sand and cool breezes. Concern was sometimes expressed about the brevity of the girls' "bathing costumes." In 1894, the *Eastern Chronicle* of New Glasgow opined that:

> The girl puts on lots of airs
> when she dips in ocean's tide.
> But we may pardon her for that,
> since she puts on little besides.

Newspaper editors of 1894 might be shocked at the "bathing costumes" of both men and women now, but what has not changed is the enjoyment of swimming in rivers, lakes, or oceans, and memories of hot summer days at the beach.

FIRST DAY ON THE ICE, THE CHEDABUCTO CURLING CLUB, 1963

The first known day of curling in Guysborough was in February 1963 on the ice of DesBarres Pond. Among the participants pictured here are Keith Ross, Sholto D. Morrison, Edgar Sceles, Frank Gosbee, Clifford J. Hawes, Ross Burry, and Al Marlowe.

Although curling has a long history in parts of Nova Scotia, the first recorded matches in Guysborough did not take place until 1963. In that year, some who had experience with curling elsewhere arranged for a game on the ice of DesBarres Pond. Interest grew rapidly and that same year an executive, which included William Shea and J. Walter MacDonald, moved quickly to erect a building on land donated by Charles Pyle just outside of Boylston. The building had a sheet plastic roof, rough boards, side hatches to regulate the temperature, and natural ice which was maintained by water pumped from the nearby brook. This building was quickly reconstructed to include two rinks, a club house, and, in about 1965, an artificial ice plant. Edgar Sceles is remembered as a moving spirit of the club, and with Earl Wright, Ken Stanway, and Al Marlow was a member of a rink that played in the provincial championships in Sydney. More recently, members of the club have brought provincial and national championship honours to their home rink.

The Guysborough District Fish and Game Association received its charter in 1930 and has been active ever since. The association purchased land and built a club house at MacPherson's Lake in 1962. It organized a "Sports Meet" at the lake that featured many contests in events like swimming, canoe races, log burling, the kettle boil, chopping, sawing, rolling pin throws, and nail driving. These boys are practising their skills on the greased pole, with varying degrees of success.Standing: David Worth, Glen Chisholm, Jerry Jamieson, James Power, Graham McAuley, Keith David. Sitting: Shawn Hadley, Early Clyde, Roy Williams, Eldon Halloran, Hal Creamer, Neil Decoff, and coach Gordon Drysdale.

THE GUYSBOROUGH JOSTS, NOVA SCOTIA INTERMEDIATE D TEAM, 1970

Baseball has been popular in Canada at least since the 1850s, and was probably introduced to the Maritimes from New England. The first ball games played in Guysborough are undocumented, but ball was likely played wherever there were children and makeshift equipment. *Brown and Gold*, the Guysborough Academy yearbook of 1932–1933, told of the Academy's 14-10 victory over Canso by the school's nine-man baseball team. Softball was also played in the schoolyard. Consequently, the *Brown and Gold* sports editor reported, "the windows on the west side have been newly and attractively screened to eliminate the danger of broken glass." Baseball games were usually played at the Athletic Association field located on Church Street and the Sunnyville Road behind Kennedy's against teams from nearby communities like Larry's River, and attracted a lot of local interest.

By the mid-1950s a group organized the Guysborough Bombers, and it was among the first of the local teams to play in provincial championships. Thereafter, softball, later called fastball, was the most popular game played in Guysborough. In the early 1960s, a local Junior League—with teams in Guysborough, Canso, Hazel Hill, and Queensport— was active. In 1966, Gordon Drysdale became the coach of a men's Intermediate team that had participated in the provincial playdowns in 1965. From 1966 to 1980, sponsored by B&G Jost, Drysdale coached the Josts, in their distinctive red and white uniforms, to a provincial Intermediate D Championship in 1970, and a provincial and Maritime Intermediate C championship in 1974. The team played in five different provinces. The largest crowd ever to attend a sporting event in Guysborough occurred when the King and His Court, a travelling five-man team, played the Josts in front of an entertained and appreciative audience.

In 1972, the Eastern Counties Softball Association had been organized, encompassing Guysborough, Antigonish, and Inverness counties. Within a year it had twenty-two intermediate and about ten junior teams registered with the Nova Scotia Softball Association, and almost one thousand people involved. The four groupings of the intermediate teams, which included one for female players, were active in many of the communities. Many local teams played in—and won—important provincial and national championships. The town still produces excellent baseball players, and in 2001, the 1981 Nova Scotia Canada Games Men's Softball Team was inducted into the provincial Sports Hall of Fame, Guysborough players Wayne Clyke, Jim Fitzpatrick (Mulgrave), Darrell Hadley and Paul Long included.

Chapter 5

Street Scenes and Domestic Architecture

GUYSBOROUGH FROM THE AIR

The streets and streetscapes of a community reveal some of its history; even more is told by an examination of its material culture. The layout of the town plot shows that Guysborough was a planned community, and the variety of architectural styles reflect both the change in what was considered fashionable and the financial resources available. In his recent work on the streets of Guysborough, Christopher Cook points out that there are seventy-eight buildings within the village that are at least one hundred years old, as well as a good number that are between one hundred and fifty and two hundred years of age. These buildings, whether commercial, institutional, or residential, are the stuff of history.

THE FOSTER HOUSE ON PLEASANT STREET, C.1890

As pioneers replaced their log houses with framed buildings, they naturally built homes in the style of those that they had left behind, and that they could afford. For many, the traditional architecture of their past was the "Cape Cod" style—a one-and-a-half storey house with a pitched roof, and sometimes dormers. The style had the advantage of simplicity and flexibility, and could be expanded either by lengthening, adding a second story, or by the adding a wing on the back in the form of an "L" or a "T."

This house, built over two hundred years ago, provides an example of the Cape Cod style. The "L" was likely a later addition, although its frame is also secured by trunnels (wooden pegs or tree-nails). The house was first clad with shingles, and evidence of a layer of birch bark between the shingle and the boards can still be found. The fir shingles used on many of the old homes and other buildings were first boiled in quick-lime, which made them almost impervious to rot. They would wear paper thin and their nails rust off before they needed to be replaced. This old house sheltered a number of families, including this author's own. It is still standing on Pleasant Street and remains a private residence. In this photograph the proud householders, Mr. and Mrs. J. H. Buckley, their two children, and the dog are all posed outside the picket fence.

LOOKING AT GUYSBOROUGH FROM THE HARBOUR ON A STILL DAY, 1891

This photograph shows more than a fisherman rowing his dory on a fine day on the harbour. Several of the buildings were to disappear over the next forty years, including the Guysborough Academy, which was replaced in 1895, and the Masonic Hall (the three-story building on the right) and Jost's Store (the four-story building in the lower centre), which were destroyed by fire—but the real story this picture tells is about the waterfront. The number of storehouses, warehouses, wharves, and piers point to Guysborough's connection to the sea. Some of the waterfront buildings would have held goods for export as well as imported items to be sold locally. Others, no doubt, held dried or pickled fish, and fresh fish to be delivered to the markets of New England via the new railway link at Mulgrave. The coastal packets to both Mulgrave and Halifax also tied up at one of these wharves, and other vessels were often moored in the safe anchorage that the harbour provided.

**AN EARLY
PICTURE OF
GUYSBOROUGH
TAKEN PRIOR
TO 1895**

The large, long, white building on the top left is the 1866 Guysborough Academy, while on the right is the structure that later generations referred to as the Provincial Building. The John J. Sangster Shipyard is at the foot of Pleasant Street and a number of buildings, residences, shops, stores, and wharves that still exist are evident. Based on the cluster of warehouses and other buildings along the waterfront, it is clear that this was the commercial heart of the village.

**THE NORTH
END OF MAIN
STREET ON A
BUSY DAY, 1933**

This picture of Main Street, looking north from the clock tower of the post office, reflects a busy day in the village. Automobiles and pedestrians stretch from Mark O'Connor's Store all the way to the post office itself.

THE GEORGE E. BUCKLEY HOUSE ON MAIN STREET, C.1900

George E. Buckley, MD, graduated from Jefferson Medical College in Philadelphia in 1867, and his name was on the list of practising doctors in Nova Scotia for over sixty-seven years. He built his family home in a modified Queen Anne style, with a two-door vestibule and veranda topped by a shared roof with a balustrade. In the early days, the view from the back of the house of the harbour included the shipyard next door, replaced in later days by the summer residence of their Tory in-laws. Dr. Buckley's office stood next to his house, and it was not unusual to see a horse and carriage waiting at the gate. When there were very few telephones in the village, Dr. Buckley had two—one in the office and one in his house. Often one of only two or three doctors in the entire county, he was constantly on-call. Stories about Dr. Buckley are still told, and they are a tribute to his years of service to the community. The house is no longer a private residence, but it still stands, without too many alterations, as it has for over one hundred years.

THE DR. EDWARD CARRITT HOUSE ON PLEASANT STREET, C.1900

Built by one of the Foster family about 1810, the simple elegant lines of this two-and-a-half storey, mid neo-Classical residence reflects architectural change and hints at either growing prosperity or a growing family. In its almost two hundred years, this house on Pleasant Street has offered shelter to a number of families, including that of Dr. and Mrs. Edward Carritt and Mr. and Mrs. Shalto Morrison. Dr. Carritt was born in 1800 in England, received his medical degree from Edinburgh, married Harriet Peacock in 1826, and came to Nova Scotia that year. He settled in Guysborough in 1842 and retired in 1884 due to the death of his wife and his own failing health. At the time of his retirement, he was the Dean of Serving Doctors in Nova Scotia. His last days were spent in Dartmouth with his daughter, far from the people and community he had served so faithfully. Hilda Cox relates that the morning he left Guysborough, feeble and with assistance, he stopped at the top of McColl's Hill and "looked all around at the places he was leaving," and knew that he would not see again. Later resident Shalto Morrison, a First World War pilot, was the High Sheriff of Guysborough County for many years.

The picket fence is not purely ornamental, and fenced animals both out and in. The several out-buildings show that barns, sheds, and stables were needed for the horse and carriage; often a cow or two and some chickens also needed to be housed. The days before indoor plumbing also meant that every house and public building had a privy as well.

THE CAPTAIN JAMES HADLEY HOUSE ON MAIN STREET, C.1900

The Captain James Hadley house provides a fine example of the Gothic revival architecture that was popular in rural Nova Scotia. Constructed around 1872, this triple-gable house, with its roofline finials and decorative chimneys, cap windows and vestibule, is impeccably symmetrical and balanced. In front of their neatly painted picket fence, the family, dressed in their Sunday best, pose for the photograph. Hadley's Wharf and warehouse were only a short distance behind the house. The wharf, one of the longest on the waterfront, was busy with ships loading and unloading, and was an endlessly fascinating spot for young boys to visit and hope they would go unnoticed. Laurier Grant remembered that there was usually something to do there, but on the occasions that they were not welcome, they "would be sent off by Capt. Jim Hadley using a hoop pole"—a slender birch or maple pole that would be split and used as hoops on barrels and undoubtedly could be a smarting impetus to a quick exit, and a deterrent to idleness. It is difficult to connect the peaceful scene in the picture to the ferocity of a fall gale, when a vessel moored at Hadley's wharf was pushed by the extreme winds and high water and ended up with its bowsprit in Captain Hadley's kitchen.

**THE ROBERT
MORRISON
HOUSE ON MAIN
STREET, C.1900**

The Gothic revival or, as termed by some "carpenter gothic" style of architecture, was commonly used and continues to be found in Guysborough residences. The style re-emerged in Britain in the late 1700s, and pattern books of house plans were readily available from British and American sources. Indeed, magazines like the *Canadian Farmer* carried an architectural section that included articles and plans for "A Cheap Farmhouse" or "A Small Gothic Cottage." Elizabeth Pacey points out that the basic elements of the Gothic-revival included a central gable with a decorative Gothic window, and a central doorway decorated with simple Gothic mouldings and flanking windows. These features are included in the house that Henry Marshall Jost built in anticipation of a marriage that never took place, although he and his widowed sister occupied the home for some years.

This picture shows the normal symmetry of the Gothic revival house, as well as the variations to the basic Gothic that it possesses. Neither the Palladian window in the central gable, nor the Scottish dormers nor the faceted windows were standard. The vestibule, with a decorative balustrade on its roof, has a side entrance, with front and opposite side windows, and is an adaptation which is better suited to the physical hillside location of the house. The three persons in this picture are likely members of the Robert Morrison family, who purchased both store and house from Henry Marshall Jost. Several generations of the family lived in this house before it was sold. It still stands on Main Street, much as it is pictured here.

THE W. H.
CUNNINGHAM
HOUSE AT MAIN
AND PLEASANT
STREETS,
c.1900

One of the common styles found in the domestic architecture of Guys-borough represents the "romantic style of the French Chateaux with their curving mansard roofs." Elizabeth Pacey points out that this form was popular in Nova Scotia from the 1870s to the mid-1890s, and it seems to have been a favourite in Guysborough. This residence, built for William H. Cunningham when he was married, reflects the features of the "Second Empire" style, as it was called in the twentieth century in honour of Napoleon III and Princess Eugenie, who began the revival of the country French fashion in architecture. The deep slope of the mansard roof is evident here. The Pleasant Street yard seems to contain a summerhouse awning, and the hedge that later domi-nated the corner is strictly under control. In the background are the Baptist Church and the Guysborough Academy. Across the corner on Pleasant Street is the home of fellow merchant Lewis Hart, with its spacious grounds and linden trees. Across Main Street is Dr. George Buckley's new house and office, and within view is John J. Sangster's shipyard. While the four occupants of the carriage are not identified, the carriage itself could have been built in Guysborough, as there were at least two carriage shops in town. Indeed, the harness could also have been made locally from leather prepared at the tan-nery about two kilometres away. While the window glass and some other items would be imported, semi-isolated communities like Guysborough were remarkably self-contained.

THE GLEBE HOUSE OF ST. ANN'S PARISH ON CHURCH STREET, C.1900

In 1880, the congregation of St. Ann's Catholic Church built a new glebe house for the resident parish priest. The style chosen was that of "Second Empire," popular in Guysborough at the time. Constructed by Thomas O'Neil, who had also built the parish church a few years earlier, it was reported to be modelled after the glebe house in Heatherton. Shown here with the long-serving Father Tomkins, the home was a model of symmetry: the bell-curved mansard roof, the dormers, the central bay portico, the roof brackets—together these provide a fine example of the French Chateaux architectural style that, after the 1890s, was less regularly used. The building was replaced in the 1970s.

LT. GOVERNOR J. C. TORY'S BELMONT FARM, c. 1910

James Cranswick Tory (1862–1944) was the son of Robert K. and Anorch (Ferguson) Tory of Port Shoreham, Guysborough County. Educated at Guysborough Academy, Wesley Theological College (Washington, DC), and McGill University (Montreal), he served as the Liberal MLA representing Guysborough from 1911 to 1925, and was the Lieutenant-Governor of Nova Scotia from 1925 to 1930. Although he lived in either Montreal or Halifax in the winter months, Tory maintained a summer home on his Belmont Farm estate on the outskirts of Guysborough.

Tory took a deep interest in the operation of a model farm on his estate, bringing one of his farm managers, Percy Moulton, from England to watch over it. While lieutenant governor, Tory gave a speech to open the Windsor Exhibition in 1929, explaining that he had been born on a farm and had kept a working farm all his life, and had cleared one of the stoniest farms in the province. Tory commented that perhaps he should be called an 'agriculturist" rather than a farmer, and explained the difference by stating: "A farmer is a man who makes his money in the country and spends it in the city; an agriculturist makes his money in the city and spends it in the country. I am afraid I have been more of an agri-culturist than a farmer." By whatever name, Tory was in tune with the turn of the seasons, with his crops, and the well-being of his herds. He also wanted a suitable home, and on the hill overlooking Cutler's Cove, with an outstanding view of both the harbour and the village, J. C. Tory built his "cottage" in a late Victorian style, incorporating a variety of architectural features. Here, behind its well-kept picket fence and new shrubs and trees, the two-storey asymmetrical summer resi-dence rose. The eclectic house was a suitable summer residence for a successful businessman, farmer, and lieutenant governor. It was destroyed by fire in the early 1920s, and Tory built a new residence on the "footprint" of this one, albeit in a different style. On his death, Tory left the house to his brother, Henry Marshall Tory, who later willed it to the community to be the core of the Guysborough Memorial Hospital.

THE DESBARRES MANOR ON CHURCH STREET

The grandest of all the private residences in the village was the home built for William Frederick DesBarres in about 1837. W. F. DesBarres was a lawyer, the son of John F. W. DesBarres and grandson of Joseph Frederick Wallet DesBarres, the latter having served as the royal governor of both Cape Breton Island and Prince Edward Island. William married a daughter of Thomas "King" Cutler of Guysborough, and established his practice in the shire town. He was elected as a Reform member of the Assembly, appointed to the Executive Council, was Judge of Probate, and served for thirty-five years as a Judge of the Supreme Court of Nova Scotia. His home reflected his social position and heritage as a prominent son of a prominent family. The house was set deep in its gardened grounds, with a circular drive, and it faced Church Street, which then led directly into the road that sometimes linked Guysborough to the rest of the province. The house was built in the mid-1830s, and for over one hundred and forty years it was owned by the DesBarres family. According to architectural historian Charles Brilivitch, the home was constructed in, or heavily influenced by, the unusual and little known Egyptian revival style.

The old house and grounds have recently been lovingly restored and enlarged by the construction of wings on each end of the original building. The original brick bake oven was uncovered in the restoration and is now in fine working order.

LOWER MAIN STREET, 1940S

Lower Main Street after 1940 is very similar to the streetscape of today. The Royal Bank of Canada building is first on the left, followed by the barbershop. Next is the Buckley shop, where two generations of Buckley watchmakers, jewellers, optometrists, and salesmen of fine china presided. The Harbour View House of Mr. and Mrs. Percy Moulton stands next to a barely visible building that alternately held a shop and private residence. Further on, separated by roads to their respective wharves, stand Jost's Store, D&M Store, and Morrison's Store. On Upper Main Street, the building on the immediate right was later the Municipal Building. The only other clearly visible building is the residence of Walter Buckley on the slope of McColl's Hill. Poles are carrying electricity to the various residences and businesses, and probably also telephone and telegraph wires.

THE FRANCHEVILLE–HEMMING HOUSE ON MAIN STREET, C.1945

Located at what is now the very end of Main Street, this home has been owned by the same family since the 1840s. Built in a late neo-classical/ Georgian tradition, the house is, in many ways, a typical two-storey home— its elegance lies in details like the three-window dormer, shuttered windows, and front-door porch with balustrade and posts. While not all of the out-buildings have survived, and there is no evidence in this photograph of the wharves and warehouses that were once part of the estate, it is obvious that the builder was a person of some wealth and position in the community. The setting of the house adds to its charm. Faced looking down the harbour toward its mouth, the progress of every vessel that came in from Chedabucto Bay could be observed. The inlet on the left side of the photograph is Miller's Cove, named in honour of Christian Miller, one of the pioneers who estab-lished Guysborough. Edmund H. Francheville, who built the house, was the nephew of Anne, wife of Christian Miller. Born in Virginia in 1810, he came to Guysborough at seven years of age, and spent the rest of his life in the town. He was the High Sheriff, Lloyd's of London Agent, Vice Consul of the United States, and a Magistrate. His home reflected his social position. One of his sons was Charles Miller Francheville, a local merchant, mariner, and politician who was elected to the Legislative Assembly as a Liberal and later appointed to the Legislative Council. Today, the home looks much as it did then, although there is no longer a public road between the house and the cove.

THE RUSSELL WILLIAMS HOME AND FARM ON GREEN STREET, c.1950

The line between town and country was largely artificial, as this picture shows a working farm well within the range of the school bell of Guysborough Academy and the Anglican Church. Many of the visible residences on Pleasant Street would also have had a stable for a driving horse, a cow byre, and a chicken coop. Before milk trucks, bread delivery, and all the conveniences of modern life, each household was much more of an independent unit. Vegetable gardens were necessary, and space had to be provided for them. The cows, chickens, goats, ducks, horses, and pigs were not pets, but rather an integral part of the family economy.

DR. GEORGE E. BUCKLEY

Dr. George E. Buckley, who served the area as a medical doctor for nearly seven decades. During his first sixty-five years, he travelled to visit his wide-spread practice on horse back, by horse and wagon, and later by car. In the last two years of his life, after recovering from a broken hip, Buckley restricted his practice to office visits only. Next door to Dr. Buckley's house was his office, where he maintained office hours. Included in his equipment was an examining chair/table, on which he could check his patients for various ailments before prescribing suitable medication and in which, after administering a couple of shots of medicinal brandy for pain relief, could pull a tooth. The total cost of the extraction and medication was twenty-five cents.

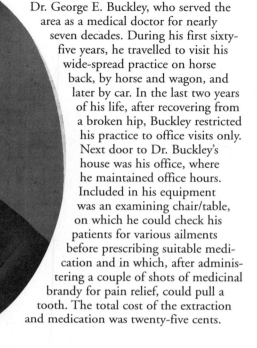

DR. GEORGE E. BUCKLEY'S EXAMINATION CHAIR

Chapter 6

Guysborough at War

1914 – 1918

A. GALLAHAN	P. FRASER
L. FRASER	W. HADLEY
R. LIPSETT	G. MARR
T. MORRIS	J. SCRANTON

1939 – 1945

S. CARR	K. GEORGE
W. GRADY	G. GREENCORN
C. HART	B. JOST
R. LAWRENCE	L. LUCAS
F. MacKENZIE	P. MacPHERSON
G. MYERS	G. MYERS
A. RYAN	M. SHEA
H. SKINNER	E. SMITH
D. SNYDER	R. ULOTH
W. WILLIAMS	

GUYSBOROUGH BRANCH 81 ROYAL CANADIAN LEGION MONUMENT

Guysborough's war casualties represent a cross-section of the community's population. People of all different race and class origins made the supreme sacrifice in defence of their families, homes, and country. During the War of 1812 between the United States and Great Britain, Fort Point, the site of the earliest French battlements, was rearmed. The local militia and later the volunteer units like the Chedabucto Greys were filled with citizen soldiers. Both World Wars, the Korean Conflict, and various military and peacekeeping responsibilities of the Canadian armed forces have been shared by the people of Guysborough.

MATRON MARGARET MARJORIE "PEARL" FRASER (1884–1918), C.1910

Behind every name inscribed on a war memorial is a story of heroism and bravery, of service and commitment. Included in the many names on the World War I monument in Guysborough are P. Fraser and L. Fraser. Pearl and Laurier Fraser, sister and brother, were the children of Duncan C. Fraser, former MP and lieutenant governor of Nova Scotia, and Bessie Graham Fraser, and siblings of Alistar Fraser, himself a wounded veteran of the war who survived and who would later become the lieutenant governor of Nova Scotia.

Margaret Marjorie "Pearl" Fraser, RN, volunteered for active service in September, 1914 and spent three years in France as a Nursing Sister in casualty clearing centres close to the front lines. On June 27, 1918, just a few months before the end of the war, she was on board the hospital ship *Llandovery Castle*, which was on a return run to England after landing 644 wounded men in Halifax. When nearing the Irish coast, despite showing the markings that protected hospital ships under international law, it was torpedoed by a German submarine and 234 of the 258 passengers and crew died. Among the causalities were Matron Margaret Fraser and the thirteen other nursing sisters on board. They had been launched in a life boat, but the boat's oars were damaged and it drifted into the sinking stern of the ship. Within eight minutes the life boat was overturned and all fourteen of the nursing sisters were lost. A survivor later wrote: "Unflinchingly and calmly as steady and collected as if on parade, without a complaint or outward sign of emotion, our fourteen devoted Nursing Sisters faced the ordeal of certain death." The unwarranted attack on the *Llandovery Castle* was deemed a war crim,e but the officer who committed it disappeared and was never brought to trial. Canadians were outraged and the little village on the bay wept for its child, another sacrifice to the war. Pearl Fraser and fellow Nova Scotian Nursing Sister Minnie Follette were commemorated in the name the Fraser-Follette Chapter of the IODE in Halifax. In New Glasgow, the Margaret Fraser Chapter of the IODE was named in honor of Matron Fraser.

In August 1914, Britain asked Germany to withdraw from Belgium, and soon thereafter war was declared, British support in Canada was strong. Among the first in Guysborough to present himself for duty was Cookson "Old Man" Dickie, who farmed at Dickie's Flats. Dickie had volunteered for militia service during the Fenian Raids of the 1860s and over fifty years later, in his old age, he was ready to serve once again. He was rejected because of his age, but if any of the stories of Dickie's abilities with a rifle are true, the recruiters might have missed their best man.

The first contingent of the Canadian Expeditionary Force sailed for England on October 30, 1914, and with them was young Roy Grant and others from the Guysborough area. These young men suffered the horrors of trench warfare and the many losses of the First World War.

GUYSBOROUGH COUNTY MEN OF THE 193RD BATTALION TRAINING IN GUYSBOROUGH, 1916

In 1916, the 193rd Battalion was authorized by the Government of Canada, and John Stanfield, MP for Colchester, was made its first commanding officer. Its territory embraced the six eastern counties of Nova Scotia including Guysborough. Within a month of its creation the battalion was over strength, and due to lack of space at the regular military bases, recruits were billeted and trained in their home counties and then assembled prior to being shipped overseas. In Guysborough, the Exhibition Grounds became the Parade Grounds, and the buildings there were used by the recruits and their officers. The 193rd was mobilized at Camp Aldershot in May 1916 and underwent additional training that summer and early fall. Reviewed by Minister of Militia Sam Hughes, Prime Minister Robert Borden, and his wife, Laura Bond Borden, the 193rd received its "Royal Blue" colours on September 26, 1916. On October 12, 1916 the 193rd embarked on the Olympic for England where the Battalion was broken up to reinforce the 185th and other Nova Scotia Battalions in the field.

The men in the photograph are not individually identified, but some of the Guysborough citizens who served in the 193rd were Privates Leo Kennedy, L. J. Barss, J. C. Jamieson, and W. McPherson; Sergeant D.W. Nelson; and Lance-Corporal D. Hendsbee.

193rd. leaving Guysborough, May 30.16. MAP Photo

THE 193RD LEAVING GUYSBOROUGH, MAY 30, 1916

Standing on the deck for one last look at home, this is the 193rd leaving Guysborough on May 30, 1916, on their way to Aldershot and, a few months later, to the battle fields of World War One in Europe.

Men from Guysborough were in other units as well, serving in the Nova Scotia Highlanders, 85th Overseas Battalion; the Cape Breton Highlanders, 185th Battalion; and the Royal Air Force. Some rose through the rank—D. B. Howard became a company quarter master sergeant, A. D. Archibald a captain, and Henry Farrell a sergeant. Others, of course, did not even return.

ADVERTISEMENT, c.1916

Of all Loyalist immigrants to Nova Scotia, a greater percentage of Blacks than Whites fought in the American Revolution. Black Nova Scotians fought in every British war thereafter and one, William Hall, won a Victoria Cross for valor in the relief of Lucknow during the Indian Mutiny of 1857. But when young Black men rushed to enlist in the World War I armed forces to serve beside their White neighbours, many of them were rejected by recruiting officers on the basis of race with notes that Black men should not be part of a "white-man's-war". However, in July 1916, an all-Black unit—the Number 2 Construction Battalion—was created, and as the available pool of manpower dwindled, Black men and White men were both faced with conscription after August 1917. Several Guysborough men, including Norman Borden, Joseph Clyke, Howard Desmond, Hartley Jackson, and James Desmond were volunteer members of the Number 2 Construction Battalion and served with distinction. Other young Black men from the area went directly into combat units, proving that they could be depended upon in front-line action. Some enlisted in the 106th Battalion, the Nova Scotia Rifles, which provided reinforcements for the Canadian Corps in the field. Race was not a recruitment issue in World War II or thereafter, and young Guysborough people of all races have regularly responded to their nation's call to arms.

Burton Jost was killed in the Netherlands on June 25, 1943. He was the son of A. C. Jost, a Guysborough medical doctor and local historian. A mining engineer, Burton Jost had to convince military authorities to accept him in the airforce. This photograph shows him on a job site in happier times.

He had completed his tour of duty as a pilot on a Halifax Class bomber and was promoted to Flight Commander and reassigned to Canada. Before he left he filled in for an ill comrade who was unable to fulfill his mission, and was hit by enemy fire over the town of Herten. He ordered his crew to bail out of the burning plane and, rather than risk the plane's crashing into the town, he attempted a landing in a nearby field. His action saved the civilian population of the area and while he was never given a medal for his feat, he was remembered by a man who as a small boy witnessed Jost's heroism, and years later wrote about it.

**LAURIER
BORDEN,
SECOND WORLD
WAR VETERAN,
1939**

Sixty people from the immediate Guysborough area served in the Second World War. Norman Skinner, a noted scrapper, joined the Cape Breton Highlanders and was killed in Italy; George Longobardi, with the West Novas, was wounded in the Italian campaign. Laurier Bordon served overseas and Andrew Johnston was a veteran as well. Joe Jamieson, whose story was recounted in *Testaments of Honour*, served with the 86 Anti-Coast Battery and the FSST in North West Europe and Italy. Leland Williams served with the RCNVR on convoy duty between Newfoundland and Ireland, and Joe MacDonald and William (Billy) Jones were also in the Navy, while Floyd Gerrior was in the Airforce and Dr. Lauder Brunton was in the Medical Corps on D-Day There are too many others to list here, but Guysborough and area certainly made a valiant contribution to the cause of the Second World War.

E-COMPANY, GUYSBOROUGH PLATOON AT THE RIFLE RANGE, GUYSBOROUGH, IN THE EARLY 1940S

Not all military service was overseas. The wars of the twentieth century developed into "total war" which influenced the entire economy and affected the whole population. While young men and women were fighting in Europe, agriculture, mining, manufacturing, and most other business and industry in Canada was directed to the military effort. On the home front there were ration books, food and gasoline shortages, metal drives, and War Bond campaigns to help raise money for the war.

The issues of home defence and recruitment were of concern to the authorities, and local companies of those too young, too old, or too essential at home to be sent overseas were created. Laurier Grant, the Postmaster at Guysborough, was "asked by the Commanding Officer of the Pictou Highlanders to raise a reserve army company in eastern Guysborough County." With the rank of 2nd Lieutenant and Officer Commanding E Company, he recruited platoon commanders and non-commissioned officers, some of them veterans of the first war, and together they enlisted troops. Soon three hundred men in platoons stationed at Guysborough, Canso, and Isaac's Harbour were in training. Officers seeking promotion wrote the regular army examinations and many of the young recruits "joined the active force on reaching the age of 18 and gave distinguished service overseas. Unfortunately a number of them did not return." The company was disbanded at the end of the war. The service of the Aircraft Detection Corps, also organized by Laurier Grant, who ended his service with rank of Major, also ended with the war. These organizations provide further examples of the involvement and sacrifice of ordinary citizens in the wartime interests of their country, an involvement that was magnified by the contribution of members of the Red Cross and other groups.

A TRIBUTE TO THE WAR EFFORT, THE HMCS *GUYSBOROUGH*, 1943

The *Guysborough* was built in Vancouver and commissioned on April 22, 1942. After serving on the west coast, it arrived in Halifax on April 30, 1943. In February 1944, after local service and a refit, the *Guysborough*, with *Canso, Kenora,* and *Wasage,* left Halifax for Plymouth, England by way of the Azores. There it was "assigned to the 14th Minesweeping Flotilla and was present on D-Day", the massive 6 June 1944 allied attack on the beaches of Normandy that opened a second front and marked a shift in the balance of the war effort. After a refit in Lunenburg, Nova Scotia, in the winter of 1945, the *Guysborough* was torpedoed and sunk with the loss of fifty-one of its crew. Although the life of HMCS *Guysborough* was only three years long, the people of the community for whom it was named can be proud of both the tribute to their hometown and of the vessel's record of service.

VICTOR SHEA, NORTH NOVA SCOTIA HIGHLANDERS, C.1944

This is Victor Shea at about twenty years of age. He wears the badge signifying his successful completion of parachute training and the flash of the North Nova Scotia Highlanders on his shoulder. He was one of the young men from Guysborough who volunteered for service in the Second World War. Many like him had followed the build-up to war in the newspaper and radio accounts that made war seem inevitable.

After the Second World War was declared, young people in Guysborough again flocked to join the armed forces. Others were employed in war industries and everyone struggled through the dark days of rationing, shortages, worry, elation, and heartbreak.

The five Shea brothers, Henry, Joe, Jerome, Victor, and William (Bill), volunteered for military service. Their father Patrick, was seriously wounded at Vimy Ridge during First World War, and died while still a young man; their mother Eva (Bates) was a British war bride left to raise five children alone.

Henry was killed in France in 1944 while serving with the Black Watch. Joe and Jerome were both serving with an anti-tank battalion in France when Jerome was wounded for the first time; luckily, Victor was visiting their unit and was able to help Jerome to safety. Victor was a member of Canada's first paratroop unit, the "North Novas" (1st Battalion, The Nova Scotia Highlanders, North), and at nineteen years of age he came ashore in the second wave of the D-Day invasion, spending the next eleven months in constant action. Victor served in four different units in the Second World War, and though he reluctantly admits that there may have been a unit as good as the North Novas somewhere, "there were none better." William (Bill) Shea's tenure in the forces was shorter as he was given a medical discharge, no doubt much to the relief of his mother. Parents gravely feared the arrival of a telegram or a visit from the clergy, as either one could carry sad news from the front.

MRS. EVA "GRAMMY" SHEA, C.1944

THE ROYAL
CANADIAN
LEGION
CENOTAPH
ON PLEASANT
STREET

Standing beside Christ Church, this memorial was erected in 1963 by the
Royal Canadian Legion, Guysborough Branch No. 81. In Guysborough,
the members of the Legion were meeting in Drouginine's store in 1951
and in 1954 they purchased a building on Main Street for their use. The
Guysborough Memorial Hospital had been named to honour Guysborough's
war dead, and in 1963 the Legion erected the cenotaph to reinforce their
memory in the community. The Legion moved into their new and current
building in 1972 and continues to serve the community from there.

Chapter 7

Locals, Visitors, and Special Events

THE TORY BROTHERS AT BELMONT HOUSE ON THE FARM, C.1937

James Cranswick, John A. and Henry Marshall (Marsh) Tory all summered in Guysborough, and maintained close connections with the community.. James C. was a business executive who lived outside of Nova Scotia for many years, but nonetheless served the area as MLA and the province as lieutenant-governor. John A., also a businessman, maintained a summer home in Guysborough, and was a supporter of the local church. Henry Marshall, or "Marsh," was one of Canada's best-known educators, and over his long life he helped change higher education in this country.

**LIEUTENANT
GOVERNOR SIR
JAMES KEMPT,
C.1820**

While there was once historical speculation about the possibility that Sir
Guy Carleton, Lord Dorchester, visited the village named in his honour,
Guysborough has enjoyed the official arrival of bishops, premiers, lieutenant-gov-
ernors, and governors general. The first such political visitor, after the departure
of the redoubtable Count Frontenac during the Chedabucto years, was that of
Lieutenant-Governor Sir James Kempt. On September 7, 1822, the government
brig *Chedabucto* landed Sir James and his party, which included Lord Frederick
Lennox, Captain Yorke, and Thomas Chandler Haliburton. The lieutenant-
governor received a twenty-one gun salute from the Sherbrooke Battery at Fort
Point, and one from the cannon that innkeeper Christian Miller kept on his
wharf. Kempt responded to the address, complimented the militia on their firing
precision, and left for Antigonish, taking Guysborough dignitaries Robert M.
Cutler and MLA John G. Marshall with him.

ROBERT M. CUTLER (1784– 1883), THE PATRIARCH OF GUYSBOROUGH, C.1875

Robert Molleson Cutler was born in Guysborough on October 9, 1784, the son of Thomas "King" Cutler and Elizabeth Goldsbury. The Cutlers were Loyalists and part of the pioneer settlers of the community, and Thomas Cutler became one of its most substantial and influential citizens. Robert, the only son of the family, was a worthy heir to his father's status and for a hundred years father and son made the name of Cutler respected. Robert, who H. C. Hart calls the patriarch of Guysborough, was a businessman and landowner. He worked for and with his father, was involved in shipping and the packet service, and became the first postmaster, an officer in the militia, an active supporter of the Anglican Church, the Custos Rotolorum (Warden) of Guysborough, a clerk of the Crown, and the Deputy Prothonotary. He served two years (1818–1820) as a Member of the Legislative Assembly supporting the Conservative party, and forty-three years (1838–1881) as a Member of the Legislative Council, the "upper house" of the Legislature. Through his business and family connections, Robert Molleson Cutler wielded a lot of influence and considerable power. While he no doubt had political foes, he was remembered as a public benefactor, and as both a credit to and pillar of his community. He died on May 1, 1883, just a few months short of his ninety-ninth birthday.

JAMES PYLE, C.1880S

One of the early summer visitors was James Pyle. A descendent of the Loyalists, he was born in 1824 to Steven and Elizabeth (Hull) Pyle of the Associated Departments of the Army and Navy. James Pyle was part of the out-migration of young people who left Guysborough for the United States. He settled in New York City, and married Heather A. Whitman from nearby Boylston, NS. Pyle created the James Pyle and Son's Company, and was the originator and manufacturer of "Pyle's Pearline" and other soap products. Mrs. Pyle died in 1921 in her ninety-fourth year, and her obituary praised the Pyles for their interest in their adopted city, and noted that their contributions to the Baptist churches there and "in their old homes in Guysboro County were exceeding generous." The Pyles maintained a physical connection to Nova Scotia as well. In 1912, the Truro Daily News recorded the death of their son James T. Pyle, who had succeeded his father as President and General Manager of the company, and wrote that Heather A. (Whitman) Pyle and her daughter Sarah had occasionally visited Truro friends "while en route to Guysboro to the scenes of the Pyle homestead of earlier days." This picture of James Pyle in the 1880s shows a successful manufacturer and businessman. He died in the mid-1890s.

REV. DR. DANIEL A. CHISHOLM (1859-1905), c.1895

The story of Father Daniel Chisholm also belongs to his birthplace of North Intervale, but he was educated at Guysborough Academy before he graduated from St. Francis Xavier University (BA 1880) and Urban College in Rome (DD 1888), and was ordained a Priest of the Roman Catholic Church. He became a Professor of Theology and Latin at St. FX in 1888, and in 1891 he was given the additional tasks of President, fundraiser, and construction superintendent of the University, as well as Rector and Bursar of the college. Although physically delicate, Chisholm worked tirelessly to fulfil the many responsibilities entrusted to him. Dr. James Cameron enumerated Chisholm's contribution to the University as including "a substantial building program, arrangements for a new congregation of sisters to care for the college's domestic needs, the impetus for a new Alumni Association" and "an affiliation agreement with St. Bernard's Academy which opened college-level courses to women," as well as generally protecting the interests of the institution. In February 1898, while on an extended trip to Florida for his health, his bishop replaced him as President of the University, and instead appointed him to St. Joseph's Parish, North Sydney. He died in 1905 at the age of forty-six.

NURSES, C.1895   This photograph of two unidentified nurses in Guysborough predates the existence of a local hospital. It is unclear if they were working in the community, or from the community, as many young women from Guysborough became nurses and worked in Halifax, Boston, or at war.

Governor General Lord Aberdeen and Lady Ishbel Aberdeen visited
Guysborough on Monday, October 4, 1897. He was known as a social crusader,
and she was deeply involved in the promotion of women's organizations. She
created the National Council of Women and, in the face of opposition from the
medical establishment, the Victorian Order of Nurses. The visit to Guysborough
was part of the Vice-Regal couple's third trip to Nova Scotia. While in
Mulgrave,.Lady Aberdeen recorded in her diary, they met D.C. Fraser, MP for
Guysborough County, who "lunched with us with his little boy Alistair and we
watched the arrival of H.M.S. Partridge which is to convey us...." On Monday
morning, the Vice-Regal party, including Duncan Fraser and son Alistair, board-
ed the gunboat *Partridge* and set out for Guysborough, where they were taken by
coach to the Academy. The *Halifax Morning Chronicle* reported beautiful weather
and a royal welcome by over one thousand people in Guysborough. "The committee in charge had expended time and money in decorating the town, and
the arches and arrangements at the high school surpassed anything seen hereto
in eastern Nova Scotia." The warden of the municipality, John M. Grant of
Milford, presided and Sheriff Alexander Maguire read an Address, to which Lord
Aberdeen made an "eloquent and most patriotic" reply which was received with
"cheers and enthusiasm." After a "shorter visit than we desired" the party depart-
ed, but "every heart was captured by this their kindly words and actions." It was,
Lady Aberdeen recorded, "a perfect day."

A CLASS AT GUYSBOROUGH ACADEMY, c.1900

These children were part of the "rising generation" that the trust fund established by the will of Matthew Welsh was designed to support. Matthew Welsh and his wife arrived in Guysborough in mid-June 1784 with the Associated Departments of the Army and Navy. Many of this group were among the last to leave New York, the final Loyalist stronghold of the American Revolution. Some were from the regular British Military, some were from colonial regiments, and others were Loyalists who had been banished by their colonial governments. Jost describes them as a "heterogeneous grouping of persons who had little but their need in common." With the others, Welsh received a grant of land in Guysborough, but as a skilled blacksmith, he established his shop and apparently prospered. He accepted apprentices, teaching them his trade in exchange for their services. Welsh died in April 1819, and in his will he provided for his apprentices and his wife, who lived until 1834. Without children of his own, but interested in children and education, he directed that upon the death of his wife all of his property should be sold, the proceeds invested, and the interest used to enable the inhabitants of the Township of Guysborough "to maintain a free Grammar or English School," or an academy if the trustees so desired, "for the benefit and advantage of the rising generation."

The trust fund that Matthew Welsh desired was established; 170 years later, it is still providing for the children of Guysborough. In 1866 the trustees of the estate loaned the Guysborough School Section No. 1 £285 to build the Academy of that year, and and the construction of the 1895 Academy building they began to make regular payments to the school authorities. The Matthew Welsh Trust Fund has also helped to build a playground and it still makes contributions to the students of Guysborough Academy in the form of awards. Matthew Welsh was likely never known outside of his own community and it is little known even within Guysborough, but the Matthew Welsh Trust Fund is likely one of the first private endowments of a public education institution in this province.

THE GUYSBOROUGH EXHIBITION, c.1900

A two-day Exhibition was held in Guysborough each autumn in the late 1800s and early 1900s. It was held for some years at the courthouse and then its organizers constructed an Exhibition Building in the area where the new school complex now stands. Captain Charles Maguire remembered the Exhibition as "not extensive" but that it "caused a lot of competition and was a gathering of the neighbours for two days." The exhibits composed, according to Capt. Maguire, "of different classes of horses and cattle, also cured fish, different kinds of vegetables, butter, cooking and whatnot," while Mrs. Cox remembered "boxes of oats and wheat, the bins of vegetables, the display of homemade jams and jellies and pickles, the hand made mats and quilts, etc., and outdoors, at the back of the building, the pens with the animals." Perhaps the interests and memories of little boys who attended the Exhibition had a different emphasis than that of little girls. The Exhibition was not exclusively agricultural as is evidenced by the fifty dollars voted by the Municipal Council in 1890 for the "Prize Fish" winner. Like today, local women erected booths and sold baked goods, and especially candy, to raise money for worthy causes. Captain Maguire credited the success of the Exhibition to its financial supporters, a group that included, among others, Stan. Lipsett, Tom Ferguson, John MacMaster, Alex MacIsaac, Thomas O'Neil, A. J. O. Maguire, and J. A. Fulton. Captain Maguire credits its decline to his impression that "when these men died, we did not have any to take their place."

UNIDENTIFIED MAN LIGHTING HIS PIPE, c.1900

With a bowler style hat and a twinkling eye, this man finds that a pipe provided a contemplative moment. The ability to keep one's pipe lit was the mark of the true pipe smoker. In wet weather, the dedicated smoker would simply turn the pipe upside down and continue to work, quite unaffected by the rain.

WILLIAM H. BUCKLEY, c.1905

William H. Buckley, the photographer who took many of the pictures used herein, was, by vocation, a watchmaker and jeweller, and ran a store on Lower Main (or Water) Street in Guysborough for many years. W. H. Buckley installed the clock in the tower of the post office, and every six days he or one of his sons wound it for the week. The entire family had broad interests, and were always deeply involved in the life of the community.

ELIZA BRODY,
c.1905

The elderly Eliza Brody sits up in bed to pose for the photographer with a young boy at her side. The Brodys (Brodey or Brodie are alternate spellings) were Loyalists and among the pioneer settlers of Guysborough. The names Jacob Brodie and Susy Brodie appear on the "Muster Roll of the Departments of the Army and Navy," and are listed as having been "set down at Chedabucto [Guysborough], June, 1784." They were very likely the progenitors of the Brody family of Guysborough.

Local sources say that Eliza Brody was married twice; first to Archibald Clyke, then to "Old" Bertie Brody. She had a number of children who left Guysborough and raised their families elsewhere.

Some of the last Brodys to make Guysborough home were Jack Brody and his family, who lived by the brook on the old road. Today, although there are connections by marriage, the name Brody is virtually extinguished in Guysborough.

PRINCIPAL MORLEY DEWOLFE HEMMEON, PH.D., 1868-1919, C.1915

Dr. Hemmeon was the principal of Guysborough Academy from 1914 to 1919. He was born in St. John, N.B. on April 1, 1868, and attended Horton Academy and Acadia University (BA, 1888). He became a teacher and was the principal of schools in Grand Pré, Chester, and Hastings before he and his wife, Emma (Lawrence), moved to Truro, where he taught history and applied mathematics at the Colchester County Academy. In 1905 he went to Harvard University, there earning both a Masters (1906) and a PhD (1908) in history.

He died at Wolfville on August 22, 1919 at fifty-one years of age. In the 1920 "Annual Report of the Superintendent of Education," Inspector A.G. Macdonald, MA, noted Hemmeon's death and remarked on the loss that it was to the Academy and to education in general and lauded Hemmeon, writing: "His scholarship was of high order, but higher still were his almost matchless gifts as a teacher. Luminous, incisive and exact in the preparation of topics, he possessed in an eminent degree that rare art in questioning that compels careful and searching thinking on the part of the student." Macdonald concluded by pointing to his lasting influence as many of Hemmeon's students had become teachers "and are destined to occupy the front ranks in the profession." This is the best epitaph a teacher could hope for and the community, the school, and the students had all benefited from his presence. Dr. Hemmeon's role in the community was especially important because so many young teachers were fleeing the province for the greater opportunities and salaries of the Canadian west that some schools were closed because none was available for hire. The Academy was fortunate in many of the personnel its Trustees were able to attract. In the early 1930s D.C. Fraser, later the inspector of schools for Pictou County, refurbished the high school laboratory and earned the respect of his students. Gordon Drysdale, later manager/owner of B&G Jost Ltd.; George Crawford, later of the faculty of Mount Allison University; J. Murry Beck, later of Dalhousie University; Verdun Saunders; Harold Feltmate; and Dorothy (Jost) Drysdale, who later taught at Havergal Girls School in Toronto, were all remembered for their contribution to education.

MUNICIPAL COUNCIL, 1917

In January 1917, the Western world was at war. Young men and women were in the trenches and hospitals of Europe, far from home as World War One wore on. Local affairs nevertheless continued to be important. Here, the Municipal Council of the Municipality of the District of Guysborough, created by provincial legislation in 1879, pauses in its deliberations for a group picture. Included, in no particular order, are most of the following: District No. 1 Duncan P. Floyd, Guysborough; Charles W. Morrison, Guysborough; District No.2 William A. Aikins, Intervale; District No.3 Charles S. Pyle, Boylston; District No.4 Reuben Hadley, Oyster Ponds; District No.5 David S. Hendsbee, Guysborough; District No.7 Samuel D. Hudson, Country Harbour; District No.11 Frederick David, Port Felix; District No.15 Wallace Burke, Drum Head; District No.16 Wallace Sangster, New Harbor; District No.17 G. Thomas Somers, Grosvenor; District No.19 Joseph W. Richards, Charlos Cove; District No.21 Edward Purcel, Mulgrave; District No.22 John Morrison, Hazel Hill. The Warden was B. J. Hadley, the Clerk was J. A. Fulton, and the Treasurer was W. H. Cunningham, all of Guysborough.

FAMILY CAMPS, c.1917

Despite living on the edge of the water and within a short distance of field and woods, a number of Guysborough people had camps, often on lakes, within a few miles of home. Sometimes used for hunting or fishing, they were also a refuge for the entire family. In this picture, the Buckley family gathered at their camp and for the photograph.

GUYSBOROUGH POULTRY CLUB, C.1918

Young people were encouraged to take an interest in hens, beyond required chores, through the creation of a Poultry Club in the village. Here the awards have been presented, the grand prize winner placed front and centre, and the other young members of the Guysborough Poultry Club pose for the official photograph.

LOBSTER, C.1915

A lobster this size was big enough to feed an entire family. The size and number of lobsters then available point to the viability of a cannery, such as Matthews and Scott's Fisheries down the shore from Guysborough.

Scene from Fort Point
Guysborough N. S.

THE SUMMER FAMILIES, C.1920S

Some of the notable individuals and families that summered in and around Guysborough included: the Findlays of Findlay Furnace Co.; Ramsay Traquair, Professor of Architecture at McGill University; Professor John B. Porter, the first Professor of Mining at McGill; the Tory brothers—Lieutenant Governor James C. Tory, academic Dr. Henry M. Tory, and businessman John A. Tory (and especially the descendants of John A. Tory), and many others. Some have had long connections to Guysborough, while others were more recently attracted to the area.

Hilda Cox wrote that "one of the highlights of our summer, when we were young, was the arrival of the Fraser family when school was over....They would come by train to Mulgrave and there take our little daily steamer to Hart's Wharf. We would see them walking to town, accompanied by cousins and friends. It was a merry party that bathed in the little cove below the house, and friends from town were always welcome." Duncan Cameron Fraser from Pictou County established a summer home when he was elected to the House of Commons, representing Guysborough County from 1891 to1904. He was made a Judge of the Supreme Court in 1904, Lieutenant Governor in 1906, and died in office in 1910. His eldest son, Alistair, enlisted with the 17th Battalion and served overseas, as did his brother, Laurier. The Fraser family suffered in World War One. Brother Laurier was killed in battle, sister Marjorie, who had become a nurse, was drowned when the hospital ship on which she was serving was torpedoed, and Alistair was severely wounded in the battle of Vimy Ridge. Alistair recovered, however, and by the end of the war, he had achieved the rank of Major, was awarded the Military Cross. After a distinguished career with Canadian National Railways, he retired in 1951. He served as lieutenant-governor of Nova Scotia from 1952 to 1958. It was he who had earlier reopened the Guysborough house, and again the family, cousins, and friends came for the summer. Lieutenant Governor Alistair Fraser made Guysborough his residence when he retired, and his sons Alistair, Ian, and Duncan, with their families and descendants, maintain their connection with this community.

HENRY MARSHALL TORY: CANADIAN EDUCATOR, 1864–1947, c.1920

Henry Marshall "Marsh" Tory was born in 1864 at Port Shoreham, educated at the local school, and later educated at Guysborough Academy. An outstanding student adept at mathematics, Tory obtained a teacher's licence and taught at home for a year to pay his first year of tuition at McGill University, from which he graduated with highest honours. Within a short time, Tory, while teaching in the university's Mathematics Department, completed a Bachelor of Divinity Degree, and then completed a Doctorate in Science (1903). He also took advanced courses in English and philosophy, and eventually was made a full professor.

Tory would become best known for his work pioneering new institutions. In 1905, he was asked by the university to undertake the creation of McGill College in Vancouver, which became the University of British Columbia in 1915. This successful venture roused Tory's pioneer instinct, and he left McGill in 1908 to become the founding president of the University of Alberta. Over the next twenty years he established the solid foundations that guided that institution to prominence. In addition, while president of the University of Alberta, Tory was prominent in creating Kharki University, established to deliver university to Canadian soldiers living in England during World War One. In 1928, at the age of sixty-five, when most are actively thinking of retirement, Tory left the University of Alberta and moved to Ottawa, where he had been invited to become the first president of the National Research Council of Canada. Tory retired after seven years at its helm, but returned to work, this time to help in creating Carleton College (later Carleton University). Tory was the college's founding president. On February 6, 1947, Tory died, as he wished, in harness. Newspapers from coast to coast mourned his passing and a colleague wrote in tribute: "For nearly 50 years Dr. Tory strode like a giant through this country and wherever he stopped he left a monument to remind us of his greatness." Tory did not forget his home area and came to Guysborough regularly. In his will, he left his summer home, "Belmont," to house a new hospital.

MEMORIAL TO HENRY MARSHALL TORY

This monument displays a plaque erected by a grateful nation to honour the memory and contribution of Henry Marshall Tory to Canada. Originally, the building behind the monument was Guysborough Academy, which was especially fitting, as Tory made such a major contribution to education in this country. After the destruction of the academy by fire in 1980, a new education building, the Cyril Ward Memorial Library, was erected on the site. No doubt Dr. Tory would be pleased.

VISCOUNT
BYNG OF VIMY,
GOVERNOR
GENERAL OF
CANADA, JULY
21, 1923

Julian Hedworth George, Viscount Byng of Vimy, was the Governor General of Canada from 1921 to 1926. He was the first governor general of Canada appointed only after formal consultation with the Canadian government. He was especially acceptable to Canada because he, although a British aristocrat and cavalry officer, was appointed to command the Canadian Corps in May 1916, and it was he who directed the Canadian attack on Vimy Ridge in April 1917. Successful where the French and British had failed, the Canadian capture of Vimy Ridge was a notable event in the military history of the country and of World War One. Byng would have been a familiar figure to some Guysborough World War One veterans, and the welcome sign and Union Jack decorating the Academy were no doubt more than a polite gesture to a visiting dignitary. Note also the presence of the pendent-bearing Boy Scouts. The Governor General of Canada has been the country's Chief Scout since 1910. The first Boy Scout Troop in Guysborough was organized in 1923, just in time for the Vice Regal visit. The troop was under the direction of Scoutmaster Rev. John Phalen, while Mrs. Phalen was the Assistant Scoutmaster. The Troop Committee included J. A. Fulton, KC (King's Council); Chairman, D.P. Floyd, KC; H.D. Cunningham, A. H. Whitman, and C. J. Francheville. The troop was registered on December 21, 1923, but was obviously active for some time before that date. Later leaders included Rev. Murray Favier, Corporal Herb Smart, and other dedicated citizens. Governor General Byng was no doubt glad to see the Boy Scouts assembled to provide an Honour Guard for his visit on July 21, 1923.

THE SOCIETY OF THE HOLY NAME PARADE, 1934

The Society of the Holy Name traces its origin to the 1274 Council of Lyons. A confraternity, or men's group, within the Roman Catholic Church, its primary purpose is to honour the Holy Name of God and Jesus Christ, and otherwise to suppress blasphemy, perjury, profanity, and improper oaths or language of any kind. This photograph portrays a procession in Guysborough on August 12, 1934, led by the clergy in their vestments, who are followed by the rest of the society. Here they are passing the post office and Cunningham Brothers' store, and they will likely will continue around town and end at St. Ann's Church.

LAURIER CRIBBEN GRANT AND MARION GRANT, C.1940

On August 15, 1896, Laurier Cribben Grant, son of George Y. and Ada Mary (Whitman) Grant, was born in Guysborough and named after Wilfred Laurier, the new Prime Minister of Canada that year. Laurier worked in the bank, operated a sawmill, and for thirty-nine years was the postmaster in Guysborough. He served king and county in both world wars. He was chairman of the Guysborough Academy Board of School Trustees from 1930 to 1948, secretary-treasurer of the Guysborough Red Cross Hospital, treasurer of the Guysborough Memorial Hospital, active in support of his political party and in a variety of other volunteer organizations and associations. He was also manager of the Guysborough Heat, Light and Power Company, a stringer for a Halifax newspaper, and a recorder of the history of the area. When he died in 1991, at ninety-four years of age, he left a considerable legacy to his community.

Conclusion

GOING HOME ON A FINE SUMMER DAY, C.1944

Turned toward home, Jean Grant (the author's mother) and her sister Dorothy Jones, with George and Jamie Grant in hand, walk along Church Street. The courthouse is on their right.

In any community, each generation is replaced by the next. The consistent factor in Guysborough has been the spirit of the place—in 220 years it has never failed to shelter, nurture, and encourage its citizens. Although some come and go, and some leave forever, the future of Guysborough seems clear: it will always be a home to its children.

Image Sources

Bryson Collection, 52
Campbell House Museum, xi
Courtesy of Stephen Grady, 2, 111, 122
Courtesy of Chedabucto Curling Club, 107
E. Hollaron Collection, 109
Francheville Family Collection, 44
Gardner Collection, 161
H. L. Grant Collection, 129, 160
J. Drysdale Collection, 66 (bottom), 133
M. MacMaster Collection, 82
Old Court House Museum, Guysborough, NS:
      Photograph Collection, xviii, 1, 14, 56, 59, 101, 124, 126, 134, 139, 156, 157
V. Shea Collection, 137
Photographs by Margaret Grant Hildebrand, 10, 127, 138, 158
All other images Nova Scotia Archives And Record Management:
      Buckley Family Fonds
      MacAskill Collection
      Dennis Collection
      Jost Collection
      Wetmore Collection

Bibliography

PRIMARY SOURCES

Nova Scotia Archives and Records Management (hereinafter NSARM) RG 5, Series P, v. 57, #86, 1830.
NSARM, MG 4, v. 345, # 14. Guysborough Registration of 1st Boy Scout Troop, 21 December 1923.
NSARM, RG 14, v. 13-14, 1812-1930. School Records Collection, Guysborough County.
NSARM, RG 5, Series P, Misc. A, v. 3, # 58. Fisheries.
NSARM, MG 100, v. 148, # 6. Guysborough Heat, Light and Power Co., Ltd.; # 7 - 7A. Anglican Church History.; # 8. Guysborough Baptist Church; v. 174, # 28. Order to hang Walter Lee.; v. 236, # 11. Sales for taxes, 1786–1796.; v. 75, # 79. Recollections of Guysborough.
NSARM, MG 3, v. 121-130. J.W. Hadley Papers.; v. 4935-4937. Hart Papers.; v. 4926-4930. Day Books–Ships.; v. 132-134. sch. Nova Zembla, 1915-1917.
NSARM, MG 9, v. 45, p. 247. Scrapbook on Counties.; v. 45, pp. 240-275. Articles on Guysborough.; v. 45. Scrapbook # 45: Guysborough: Probate Court.
NSARM. RG 5, Series GP.; v. 7, # 78. Mulgrave-Guysborough Ferry c. 1884.
NSARM. MG 4, v. 36. Guysborough Town History (1933).
NSARM, Vert. Ms. File. Guys.–Hotels–Grant's Hotel
NSARM, RG 8, v. 10, # 6. Agricultural Papers: Guysborough County, 1820.
NSARM, RG 5, Series P: v. 58, # 203.; v. 7, # 52, Request for Licence-Tavern, 1839.; v.

8A, #77, Guysborough Library, 1844.; v. 44, # 39, Petition for a Lighthouse.; v. 120, # 49, Edward Morgan Mill, 1824.; v. 57, # 86, # 149, Request for the Establishment of a Packet, 1830; v. 77, Petitions: Education, 1861.; v. 13, # 58. Town Hall Incorporation.; v. 57, 124, 146, 159. N. Brown Inn at Guysborough, 1833.; v. 57, # 91, 94, 107-108A. Request for funding for ferry to Arichat, 1830.; v. 58, # 12. Request for a ferry to Manchester. 1853.; v. 45, # 160. Guysborough Board of Health, 1850. # 82. Petition to recover damages, 1844; v. 44, # 63, Guysborough Mechanics Institute, 1843.; v. 22, # 4, Female Suffrage Petition, 1918.; v. 6, # 2, Petition of Guysborough and Manchester Temperance Society, 1835.; v. 19, # 10, # 53, # 69, Petitions Opposing Confederation.; v. 56, # 49, Grist Mill Shortage, 1917.

NSARM, RG 44, Box 44, Schools.
NSARM, RG 22, v. 36, # 13. Guysborough County Militia.
NSARM, RG 39 "C" v. 1 & 2. Supreme Court, Guysborough Co. 1836–1923.
NSARM, RG 1, v. 264, # 74. Plan of New Guysborough Road, 1854.
NSARM, MG 7, v. 123. Ship/Shipping out of Guysborough.
NSARM, MG 17, Colleges and Universities (Nova Scotia College of Art) vols. 10–11B.
NSARM, RG 5, Series A, v. 2 # 130. Petition for Court of Common Pleas, 6 December 1784.; # 34. Petition for roads, 17 June 1786.

NEWSPAPERS:

Halifax: *Morning Chronicle*, 1897; New Glasgow: *Eastern Chronicle*, 1897, 1873; Antigonish: *The Casket*; Truro: *The Daily News* 1912, 1921; Guysborough: *Guysborough Gazette*, 1895; Halifax: *Herald*, 1883, 1902; Halifax: *Acadian Recorder*, 1857, 1916; Canso: *Canso Breeze*, 1968; Halifax: *Mail/Star*, 1949; Halifax: *Novascotian*, 1858; Goshen: *Guysborough Journal*

Belcher's Farmer's Almanac, 1879–1930
McAlpines Nova Scotia Directory, 1902
Antigonish and Sherbrooke Telephone Co. Ltd. *Subscriber's Directory and Schedule of Rates.* 1909.

SECONDARY SOURCES

Aberdeen, Lord and Lady. *We Twa: Reminiscences of Lord and Lady Aberdeen.* London: Collins, 1925.
Archibald, Margaret E. *By Federal Design; The Chief Architect's Branch of the Department of Public Works, 1881-1914.* Ottawa: Environment Canada, 1983.
Army Historical Section. *The Regiments and Corps of the Canadian Army.* Ottawa: Queen's Printer, 1964.
Bird, W.R. "The Story of Nova Scotia's Highways." An unpublished manuscript in the Collections of the Nova Scotia Historical Society. Presented 7 January 1944.
Buckley, Fred. *The Last 100 Years as Seen by the Buckleys of Guysborough.* Typescript. October, 1981. 30 pages.
Burroughs, Peter. "Lucius B. Cary, 10th Viscount Falkland," *Dictionary of Canadian Biography*, v. XI (1881-1890), pp. 155-156.
Cameron, J.D. *For the People: A History of St. Francis Xavier University.* Montreal: McGill-Queen's University Press, 1996.

Campbell, Duncan. *Nova Scotia in its Historical, Mercantile and Industrial Relations.* Montreal: John Lovell, 1873.

Coleman, Margaret. "Trading History of Guysborough (Chedabucto), NS." July. 1966, pp. 74-95, in National Historic Parks and Site Branch, *Manuscript Report Number 107: Miscellaneous Historical Reports on Sites in the Atlantic Provinces.* Government of Canada: Department of Indian and Northern Affairs: Parks Canada.

Cook, Christopher A. *Along the Streets of Guysborough.* Second Edition. For the Author, 2003.

Corbett, E.A. *Henry Marshall Tory: Beloved Canadian.* Toronto: Ryerson, 1954.

Cox, Hilda. *As I Remember It.* Typescript, 39 pages, nd., [1964].

Drysdale, J. Gordon. *Characters: Including Me.* Hantsport, NS: Lancelot Press, 1984.

Evans, R.D. "Stage Coaches in Nova Scotia, 1815–1867." *Chronicles of the Nova Scotian Historical Society,* v. 24, (1938) pp. 107-134.

Fenerty, E.L. "Old Mail Routes and Post Routes of Nova Scotia: Its Highways and Byways." An unpublished manuscript in the collections of the Nova Scotia Historical Society. Presented 11 January 1911.

Fergusson, Charles Bruce, *A Directory of the Members of the Legislative Assembly of Nova Scotia,* 1758–1958. Halifax: The Public Archives of Nova Scotia, 1958.

Fergusson, Charles Bruce, ed. *Place Names and Places of Nova Scotia.* Halifax: The Public Archives of Nova Scotia, 1967.

Fergusson, Charles Bruce. *Mechanics' Institutes in Nova Scotia.* Halifax: Public Archives of Nova Scotia, 1960.

Fergusson, Charles Bruce. *The Inauguration of the Free School System in Nova Scotia.* Halifax: Public Archives of Nova Scotia, 1964.

Forbes, E.R. and D.A. Muise, eds. *The Atlantic Provinces in Confederation.* Toronto and Fredericton: University of Toronto Press/Acadiensis Press, 1993.

Forbes, Ernest R. "Consolidated Disparity: The Maritimes and the Industrialization of Canada during the Second World War." *Acadiensis,* v, XV, n.2, (Spring, 1986), pp. 3–27.

Francis, R. Douglas, Richard Jones, Donald B. Smith. *Origins: Canadian History to Confederation.* Toronto: Holt, Rinehart and Winston, 1988.

Grady, Patricia and Laureen O'Halloran. *An Historical Sketch of Guysborough Municipal Council: 1879-1978.* Typescript, n.p. [25 pages], 1978.

Grant, James W. "Frozen Toes and the Sport of Kings." *Guysborough Journal,* 20 March 1997, p. 9.

Grant, John N. "William Campbell: The Man and the Monument". *Canada: An Historical Magazine.* V.3, n.3, (March, 1976), pp. 48-57.

Grant, John N. *The Courthouses and Jails of Guysborough.* Guysborough, NS: Guysborough Historical Society, 1973.

Grant, John N. "Francis Cook." *Dictionary of Canadian Biography,* v. 1X, pp. 151-152.

Grant, Laurier C. "Private Enterprise in Guysborough, Nova Scotia." *The Nova Scotia Historical Quarterly,* v.6, n.4 (December, 1976), pp. 391-404.

Grant, Laurier C. *History of Guysborough Hospital, 1939-1965.* Typescript, 10 pages, nd.

Grant, Laurier C. "Recollections of a Life in Guysborough." Typescript. 122 pages. January 1987

Guysborough Academy. *Brown and Gold.* V.1, June, 1933 and v. 2, 1934.

Hale, C.A. *Publicly Funded Schools in Nova Scotia, Pre 1930s: Interim Report.* Parks Canada Research Bulletin, 33 pages, December, 1983.

Haliburton, Thomas C. *An Historical and Statistical Account of Nova Scotia, in Two Volumes.* Halifax: Joseph Howe, 1829.

Halliday, Hugh A. "There Auto Be a Law," *Horizon Canada.* pp. 2636-2640.

Hart, Harriet Cunningham. *History of the County of Guysborough, Nova Scotia.* (University of King's College Akins Historical Prize Essay, 1877). Belleville, Ontario: Mika Publishing, 1975.

Heathcote, Blake. *Testaments of Honour: Personal Histories of Canada's War Veterans.* Toronto: Doubleday, 2002.

Hunt, M.S. *Nova Scotia's Part in the Great War.* Halifax: The Nova Scotia Veteran Publishing Co., 1920.

Inness, Lorna. "Infamous War Crime: The German Attack on the Hospital Ship Llandovery Castle Shocked the Nation in 1918." Halifax: The *Sunday Herald.* Sunday, October 12, 2003, Section C, p8.

Jephcott, C.M. et. al. *The Postal History of Nova Scotia and New Brunswick, 1754-1867.* Toronto: Sessions, 1964.

Johnston, Angus Anthony. *A History of the Catholic Church in Eastern Nova Scotia: Volume I 1611–1827.* Antigonish, NS: St. Francis Xavier University Press, 1960.

Johnston, Angus Anthony. *A History of the Catholic Church in Eastern Nova Scotia: Volume II 1827–1880.* Antigonish, NS: St. Francis Xavier University Press, 1971.

Jost, A. C. *Guysborough Sketches and Essays.* Kentville, NS: Kentville Publishing Company, 1950.

Jost, A. C. and J.A. Morrison. *Historic Canso.* Issued Under the Auspices of The Town Council of Canso And the Canso Board of Trade. Canso, 1928.

MacDonald, Bruce. *The Guysborough Railway, 1897-1939.* Antigonish, NS: Formac, 1973.

MacKay, Donald C. *Portraits of a Province, Artists and their Pictures in Nova Scotia 1605–1945.* Unpublished Manuscript.

MacKenzie, A.A. *Guysborough County.* Typescript, 10 pages, nd.

MacPherson, Ken and Ron Barrie. *The Ships of Canada's Naval Forces 1910-2002.* St. Catharines: Vanwell, 2002.

MacNutt, W.S. *The Atlantic Provinces: The Emergence of Colonial Society, 1712-1857.* Toronto: McClelland and Stewart, 1965.

Maguire, Charles and Nina Maguire. "Memories of Guysborough." Guysborough, NS, 28 August 1962, Typescript.

Marble, Allan E. *Nova Scotians at Home and Abroad.* Windsor, NS: Lancelot Press, 1977.

Maritime Merchant. "…In Business for More Than a Century." *The Maritime Merchant.* (2 March 1944), pp. 11 and 32.

Martin, J. Lynton. *The Ross Farm Story: A brief history of agriculture in Nova Scotia with particular emphasis on life on the small upland farm.* Halifax, NS: Nova Scotia Museum, 1974.

Nicholson, G.W.L. *Canada's Nursing Sisters.* Toronto: Hakkert, 1975.

Parks, M.G. ed. *Joseph Howe Western and Eastern Rambles: Travel Sketches of Nova Scotia.* Toronto: University of Toronto Press, 1973.

Pacey, Elizabeth and Alvin Comiter. *Landmarks: Historic Buildings of Nova Scotia.* Halifax: Nimbus, 1994.

Penny, Allen. *Houses of Nova Scotia: An Illustrated Guide to Architectural Style Recognition.* Halifax: Formac and The Nova Scotia Museum, 1989.

Province of Nova Scotia. *Report of the Inspector of Rural Telephone Companies.* Halifax, NS: Minister of Public Works and Mines, Kings Printer, 1928

Province of Nova Scotia. *Annual Report of the Superintendent of Education for Nova Scotia for the year ended 31 July* 1865. Halifax: Kings Printer, 1966. Also see 1892-1906 and 1919.

Purcell, Colin and Leo Purcell. *Along the Shore Road.* For the Authors, 1996.

Quinpool, John. *First Things in Acadia: The Birthplace of a Continent.* Halifax: First Things Pub., 1936

Reid, John G. *Acadia, Maine, and New Scotland: Marginal Colonies in the Seventeenth Century.* Toronto: University of Toronto Press, 1981.

Reid, John G. *Six Crucial Decades: Times of Change in the History of the Maritimes.* Halifax: Nimbus, 1987.

Ruck, Calvin W. *Canada's Black Battalion: No. 2 Construction, 1916–1920.* Halifax: The Society for the Protection and Preservation of Black Culture in Nova Scotia, 1986.

Sager, Eric W. and Lewis R. Fischer. *Shipping and Shipbuilding in Atlantic Canada, 1820–1914.* Historical Booklet No. 42. Ottawa: The Canadian Historical Association, 1986.

Saywell, John T., ed. *The Canadian Journal of Lady Aberdeen, 1983-1898.* Toronto: The Champlain Society, 1960.

Smith, Michael. "Graceful Athleticism or Robust Womanhood: The Sporting Culture of Women in Victorian Nova Scotia, 1870-1914." *Journal of Canadian Studies*, v. 23, n 1 & 2 (Spring, 1988), 120-137.

Spicer, Stanley T. *Maritimers Ashore and Afloat: Interesting People, Places and Events Related to the Bay of Fundy and its Rivers.* Vol. I, Hantsport, NS: Lancelot Press, 1993.

Spicer, Stanley T. *Masters of Sail: The Era of Square-rigged Vessels in the Maritime Provinces.* Toronto: Ryerson, 1968.

Stephens, David E. *Iron Roads: Railways of Nova Scotia* Windsor, NS: Lancelot, 1972.

Thomas, Christopher A. "Thomas Fuller." *Dictionary of Canadian Biography*, v. XII, [CD-ROM].

Thornton, Patricia A. "The Problem of Out-Migration from Atlantic Canada, 1971-1921: A New Look." *Acadiensis*, v. XV, n.1, (Autumn, 1985), pp. 3-34.

Tory, James C. *Addresses Delivered by Hon. James Cranswick Tory, LL.D.* Ottawa: Mortimer, 1932.

Tulloch, Judith. *Dictionary of Canadian Biography*, v. VIII, pp. 223-224.

Watt, Heather. *Silent Steels: Cycling in Nova Scotia to 1900.* Halifax: Nova Scotia Museum, 1985.

Whidden, D. G. *Nova Scotia's Telegraphs, Landlines and Cables.* Wolfville, NS: Acadian Reprint, 1938.

Young, A.J. *Beyond Heros: A Sport History of Nova Scotia.* Vol. 1. Hantsport, NS: Lancelot Press, 1988.

Zinck, Jack. *Ship Wrecks of Nova Scotia.* Vol.1. Windsor, NS: Lancelot Press, 1975.

Nominal Index

Howe, Joseph xii, xiii, xxi, 28, 29, 38, 48, 84, 100, 102, 105, 166
Hudson, Samuel D. 153
Hugh, Hugh 48
Jackson, Hartley 132
Jamieson, J. C. 130
Jamieson, Joe 134
Johnson, Rollie 47
Jones, Bernice 54
Jones, Clyde 14
Jones, Eric 54
Jones, Gordon 54
Jones, Harry 96
Jones, Helen 54
Jones, Lindsay 14
Jones, William (Billy) 134
Jost, Burton 15, 66, 85, 133
Jost, Christopher iv, 45, 65, 66, 67, 165, 167
Jost, George 15, 66
Jost, Henry Marshall 4, 59, 67, 118
Jost, John 67
Kempt, James 102, 140
Kennedy, Arthur 96
Kennedy, Leo 96, 130
Larabee, Jim 96
Lawlor, John E. 53
Leet, Joseph 14
Lodge, James 28
Long, Mike 14
Longobardi, George 134
MacDonald, Joe 134
MacDonald, Walter 14, 107
MacIntyre, John 71, 81
MacIsaac, Alex 147
MacKay, Keith 107
MacKeen, Charles iv, 63
MacKeen, Robert 69
MacKinnon, Patricia 96
Maguire, A. J. O. 147
Maguire, Charlie 59, 74, 95
Marlowe, A. 107
McColl, Duncan 24
McGregor, Margaret 51
McIsaac, W. B. 17
McKay, Jean 18
McKeough, William 57
McPherson, W. 130
Miller, Christian xii, 42, 48, 124, 140
Moir, William 51, 65
Morgan, Henry 57
Morrison, Charles W. 153
Morrison, John 153
Morrison, Robert 67, 71, 118
Morrison, Shalto 116

Morrison, Sholto D. 107
Morrow, Ben 62
Morrow, John 100
Moulton, Percy 68, 121, 123
Nelson, D.W. 130
Newton, Charlotte 16, 89, 90
O'Connor, Ann 54
O'Connor, Ronnie 54
O'Neil, Thomas 147
Parker, B. L. 105
Peart, W. S. 103
Peart, Went 96
Phalen, Joe 54
Phalen, John 159
Porter, John B. 156
Purcel, Edward 153
Purcell, Colin 32
Purcell, Leo 32
Pyle, Charles S. 153
Pyle, James 142
Randall, Elisha 2
Richards, Joseph W. 153
Roberts, Charles 57
Sangster, John J. 56, 58, 92, 114, 119
Sangster, Wallace 153
Sceles, Edgar 107
Scott, George 18, 34
Scott, Moses 33
Shea, Eva 137
Shea, Henry 137
Shea, Jack 96
Shea, Jerome 137
Shea, Joe 137
Shea, Patrick 137
Shea, Victor 137
Shea, William 96, 137
Skinner, Norman 134
Smart, Herb 159
Smith, Jack 78
Somers, G. Thomas 153
Tory, Henry Marshall 19, 121, 157, 158, 165
Tory, James Cranswick 92, 121, 167
Tory, John A. 92, 95, 156
Traquair, Ramsay 156
Welsh, Matthew 146
Whitman, Heather A. 142
Whitman, William 69
Williams, Leland iv, 14, 134
Worth, Bernard 14
Wright, Earl 67, 107
Young, John 100
Young, Ralph 14